# Beyond the Covid Shock:
# The Great Economic Transition

Darryl J. Mitry, Ph.D.
&
Thomas Matula, Ph.D.

BeyondTheCovidShock.com

All rights reserved. Except for brief quotations, no part of this publication may be reproduced or used in any form or by any means graphic, electronic, or mechanical including photocopying, recording, information storage or retrieval systems, without permission in writing from the authors and holder of copyright.

Copyright 2020

Published 2021

Cover design: PROBA Graphics, Jenny Matula

PROBA Research Analytics Publication

Authors contact: identified in book, and on the website "BeyondTheCovidShock.com"

*The authors express sincere appreciation to all the readers that provided comments on this book, and special gratitude is due Cynthia Buchanan for her most helpful editing observations and clarifications.*

## The Authors
### Dr. Darryl J. Mitry, Ph.D.

Professor D. J. Mitry earned his doctorate in Economics from the University of Southern California where he received several awards including the highest Honor of Distinguished Merit. Over the years, Dr. Mitry has served on the faculty of a number of universities and has been an invited professor and speaker to communities around the world. Professor Mitry previously served as university department Chair and program director coordinating 180 faculty members and directed business and economic programs for 24 campus sites in 11 metropolitan areas. He was an early progenitor of technology for distance-education, and pioneered programs for Internet communication and delivery. Notably Dr. Mitry directed and launched the first online MBA program in the world.

Later, during 2000-2001, collaborating with Dr. Thomas Matula, they formed a company and designed a large educational program for national distribution. Together, they greatly enjoyed working with the legendary astronaut Dr. Buzz Aldrin. In 2003-2004, Dr. Mitry was selected as a United States Fulbright Senior Scholar and served as an "academic cultural ambassador" to Ukraine.

In 2005, Dr. Mitry forecast a serious downturn for the real estate market to begin in 2007, which he believed would coincide with a financial crisis. Therefore, he sold all his real estate holdings at the top of the market, and he decided to retire from fulltime teaching. In 2016-2017, he was again selected by the U.S. State Department's Fulbright program to visit the countries of Belarus, Moldova and the republic of Transnistria, where he met and spoke to business associations, public and educational communities.

Professor Mitry has won awards for teaching, research, and publication. He has served as director, investigator, and consultant to many institutions, and a "fellow" of professional societies. He has published numerous articles in academic journals and presented many professional conference proceedings. His research has often involved global assessments, and he continues to research, write, and publish. He believes that the search for truth must be the primary objective of education. He calls it the *"Prime Equation"* where:

**Truth = Reality = Accuracy = Legitimacy.**

## Dr. Thomas Matula, Ph.D.

Dr. Thomas Matula is a Tenured Professor at Sul Ross State University, Texas. He earned both his Ph.D. in Business Administration and MBA from New Mexico State University. Dr. Matula has served full time on the faculties of National University, the University of Houston-Victoria and Great Basin College while also teaching as an adjunct instructor at American Intercontinental University, Trident at AIU, and California International Business University.

Over the last thirty years he has developed several graduate and undergraduate degree programs including, in 1999, the first Masters in Ecommerce at National

University. Dr. Matula believes in a multidisciplinary approach to business strategy that integrates economics, history, and technology, providing exciting forward-thinking programs. A futurist, he has applied the principles of business strategy and economic development to write numerous academic papers on ecommerce, online education, and the emerging field of space commerce.

Recognizing that the more you understand the past the better prepared you will be for the future he integrates economic history into both his academic publications and his classes. Dr. Matula believes that the future is only a mystery to those who fail to understand the past. Similarly, the Post Pandemic Economy will be a surprise to those who are unfamiliar with the recent trends and economic history.

Email: ProfMatula@gmail.com

Website: **BeyondtheCovidShock.com**

# Table of Contents

| | |
|---|---|
| **THE AUTHORS** | III |
| **TABLE OF CONTENTS** | VII |
| **CHAPTER 1** | 1 |
|     INTRODUCTION | 1 |
| **CHAPTER 2** | 11 |
|     PANDEMICS AND ECONOMIC HISTORY | 11 |
| **CHAPTER 3** | 25 |
|     THE 2020 COVID-19 PANDEMIC | 25 |
| **CHAPTER 4** | 47 |
|     ECONOMIC TRENDS & COVID | 47 |
| **CHAPTER 5** | 61 |
|     LIFESTYLES AFTER THE COVID SHOCK | 61 |
| **CHAPTER 6** | 87 |
|     INDUSTRY -TRANSPORTATION, TRAVEL AND HOSPITALITY | 87 |
| **CHAPTER 7** | 111 |
|     INDUSTRY - RETAILING, ENERGY, INTERNET SERVICES, AND ROBOTICS | 111 |
| **CHAPTER 8** | 131 |
|     EFFECT ON HUMAN GEOGRAPHY | 131 |
| **CHAPTER 9** | 149 |
|     UNDERSTANDING THE ECONOMICS BEHIND THE BIG PICTURE | 149 |
| **CHAPTER 10** | 171 |
|     CONCLUDING REMARKS | 195 |
| **REFERENCES & SELECTED READINGS** | 198 |
|     FOR READERS' PERSONAL NOTES | 225 |
|     FOR READERS' PERSONAL NOTES | 226 |

# CHAPTER 1

## Introduction

The authors of this book have published numerous academic articles on business strategy, economics, ecommerce, and online learning throughout their long careers as scholars. They have used this knowledge to analyze and understand how the Covid-19 Pandemic has interacted with existing economic tendencies and trends to generate a new Post Pandemic Economy. The purpose of this book is to share their insights with the public. This is an easy book to read and to remember the valuable points of interest. You will not only see into the future, but you will understand how and why it is different from the daily life you lived before. As you learn about what takes place in the Post Pandemic era and what evolves to become the "New Normal" you will be able to see significant opportunities to make life choices that benefit you.

This book focuses on an Economic analysis of the changes that took place in the year 2020, when the Covid-19 Pandemic struck, and how the reactions to the Pandemic causes significant changes in the overall economy, which leads to what eventually becomes the "New Normal." The book explains how the changes provide you options for new lifestyles and productive work environments during the Great Economic Transition.

There are three important reasons to read this book:

1) You will learn how the economy in which you live is changing.
2) You will understand how the Post Pandemic economy develops from prevailing economic trends.
3) You can discover personal opportunities for success in the choices you will need to make.

Chapter 2 describes the history of pandemics, and how events changed the lives of the people that survived. The background is important for understanding the impact that operates in economic systems.

Chapters 3, 4 and 5 discuss the recent Covid-19 Pandemic of the year 2020, and the authors illustrate how people will be working in the new Post Covid Shock Economy and the inevitable lifestyle changes that take place throughout the Great Economic Transition.

Chapters 6 and 7 analyze the impact of the "Covid Shock" on the Transportation, Travel, Hospitality, Retailing, Energy, Internet Services, and Robotic industries in the United States.

Chapters 8 and 9 describe the principle economic forces that always operate behind the scenes, and the chapters describe how the projected trends will remake our cities, suburbs and rural areas.

In chapter 10, the last chapter of the book, the authors illustrate how individuals can plan to benefit from the opportunities that develop during the great economic transition to the new Post Pandemic economy. The discussion focuses on how individuals can identify their best actions for fulfilling their objectives and take advantage of opportunities during the Great Economic Transition.

The book provides a meaningful look into the future. The purpose is to give the reader information about the changes that are likely in the Post Pandemic way of life, the time of what will become the "New Normal" as the nation adapts to the Covid-19 virus. Essentially this book serves as the story of a tomorrow yet to come, but soon to arrive and evolve.

Most important, you will be better informed and better able to make the correct decisions that help you to be successful in the Post Pandemic Great Economic Transition. Throughout this book, you will learn what the Post Pandemic world will be like in the coming "New Normal." Exactly how you apply this knowledge depends on who you are, and how you react to learning about the changes described in this book. Some people will react with excitement and choose to prepare for the future and to find the opportunities for enhancing their lives. Others will react with fear and worry, and choose to complain, but in reality, there is no reason to be fearful. The authors view the future described here as an open door to a fuller and more enriched life for you and your family.

The analysis and predictions in this book focus on the American economy for two reasons. First, as a **free-market economy** it will be able to adapt to the Post Pandemic world quicker and more efficiently than government-planned economies do. This is because free market economies automatically can determine which business models and local government policies work and which do not work.

As individuals, we are both producers and consumers of products and services. Producing and consuming are competitive market-based contests of opportunity aimed at reaching the highest level of fulfillment. Participation in the contests secures the optimal possible outcomes arising from various talents, training, knowledge, and individual capabilities.

By contrast, **planned economies** depend on the decisions of a limited number of "experts" necessarily working from incomplete and usually outdated data. These "expert" bureaucrats then determine which business models and local government policies believe are winners. The plans are then directed by the governing authorities and imposed on the citizens. A government-planned system often forces the economy into directions that prevent it from effectively and efficiently adapting to inevitable changes that arise naturally by external forces. The bureaucratic experts also tend to make decisions that are based on either preserving the existing status quo of the economy or forcing it into a direction they believe is desirable, instead of allowing the economy to find its new stability from the process of millions of individuals making their own decisions based on their needs and preferences.

America has a strong tradition of both entrepreneurship and grass roots decision making. Most Americans usually do not wait for the government to tell them what to do, but will instead decide for themselves. Business owners, who find their businesses failing in one region because of government policies, will leave and start a new business in another region where the conditions are more favorable to them. Most individuals will not remain indefinitely where life is difficult or where entrepreneurism is stifled and jobs are few, but they will move to where opportunity is recognizable and where they are able to enjoy an enhanced lifestyle. This mobility of both the American labor force and the adaptability of entrepreneurs have been the defining features of the American economy, and these are the features we have already seen at work in the most recent Pandemic.

It is the freedom and flexibility of Americans to adapt in a crisis that makes it possible to analyze and predict the nature of the Post Pandemic Economy in America better than elsewhere in the world. It will also be the reason that the American economy, and its success in adapting, could serve as the role model for the economies of other nations.

The reaction of a population to a threat like the Covid-19 virus is based on how individuals see the world. In response to the virus, we have been forming new habits and behavior patterns. Many of these will persist into the Post Pandemic world, because not only we have embraced new habits but also because adapting has proven to be more beneficial than our behaviors were before the Pandemic struck. As shown in this book, these phenomena form the basis of the Great Economic Transition and the new economy, the result of accelerating economic trends, several of which existed before the Covid-19 virus struck the world.

In other words, the reaction to the viral Pandemic empowers and accelerates certain tendencies and trends that existed prior to the Pandemic. Likewise, some other previous trends will die away. Together this combination of accelerated existing and new economic trends, with the reversing and redirection of others, will create the major thrust to develop fully the Great Economic Transition to the Post Pandemic Economy.

This book will provide you with an outline of the shape of the Post Pandemic economy so you will be better able to prepare for it. The Post Pandemic era is the Great Economic Transition and it will require that you adapt to it, which means that you should prepare yourself to recognize fully the beneficial alternatives versus the inferior in order for you to make the best choices. This need not be a very difficult problem because life requires choices and individuals make them numerous times every day. The choices you make can be the correct ones, if you are equipped with some foreknowledge of events. In this way, you are apt to make optimal choices, and not suffer the consequences of poor choices or lack of action. The saying, "business as usual" implies inertia, the Post Pandemic economy is a dynamic system of change, as we observe in aspects of nature.

**At every stage of life, events are being interpreted by what individuals are thinking. The authors of this book hope it will help you to discover opportunities for avoiding undesirable consequences, and instead take advantage of fortunate prospects and new developments on the horizon.**

To use the analogy of computers, our thinking process is controlled by the programs that exist in our minds. A perfectly good analogy of our brain is that it is a super-computer, and everything that you observe is processed by its organic electrochemical software. Events that you face are processed either correctly or incorrectly. Furthermore, our perception of "self" is manufactured by the processes in our brain.

An important truth about computers is subsumed by saying, "garbage in, garbage out." If weak or inadequate data is loaded into the computer, the end result is also weak and inadequate. The same thing is true in your super-computer-brain; poor information (data) will produce poor results. Everyone that you have ever met contributes bits and pieces of data to your brain's software programs. These bits and pieces may be intentionally delivered or passively and unintentionally provided, but they are all extremely important. Frequently, these bits and pieces are unknowingly acquired, but they are always stored within your super computer's physical memory. The brain takes the data and uses a thought process (your software) to interpret the meaning of the information. The whole process is comprised of the thoughts we have stored in our memories as we are confronted with the new information.

Some of the "software programs" of our minds are impressed upon us in adulthood, but others begin even before birth, and expand in our childhood. For example, most often we have parents that assisted in creating some of our early software programs, including attempts to enhance our ability to think logically. The results of all the events that we have processed are stored in our memories, much like the hard drive of our computational machines that hold information. The software operates as thought patterns and remains unchanged unless you deliberately make changes. This book is intended to provide you with a framework for successful decision-making in the Great Economic Transition to a "New Normal."

To summarize, here are single sentence descriptions of each of the following Chapters 2 through 10.

Chapter 2 presents an overview of some past Pandemics, particularly the 1918 Pandemic and the economic consequences that show how societies changed as a result.

Chapter 3 discusses the recent Covid-19 Pandemic, the year 2020, and the natural reaction of the economy to changes and disruptions by the Pandemic.

Chapter 4 shows how Covid-19 has altered the labor force and the workplace with the underlying details for the evolution that creates the development of the Post Pandemic Economy.

Chapter 5 examines some of the inevitable lifestyle changes that accompany the shift stimulated by the Post Pandemic Economy.

Chapter 6 analyzes how Transportation, Travel and Hospitality industries will change in the Beyond Covid Shock Economy.

Chapter 7 discusses the Retailing, Energy, Internet Services, and Robotic Technology industries.

Chapter 8 shows how the projected trends will remake our Human Geography, and the consequences for the cities, suburbs and rural areas.

Chapter 9 explains how we understand the "Big Picture." Sociologically, as it were, as well as through the lens of the largely market based economy.

Chapter 10 describes how to make your plan in order to maximize your success in what becomes the "New Normal" during the Great Economic Transition.

# CHAPTER 2

## Pandemics and Economic History

For most readers of this book, the following discussion, mostly concerned with economic reactions to historical pandemics will be interesting and helpful because it illustrates how past pandemics resulted in all new modes that produced new economic opportunities. Learning about the past pandemics helps readers of this book to understand how such worldwide events result in the development of drastically changed economies. On the other hand, a few readers might already be well versed in this history and have previously realized exactly how and why such economic changes arise. Readers will know in which category they reside and will react accordingly.

## Background to Covid-19

In late fall 2019 the first reports emerged from Wuhan, China of a population seriously ill from a new unknown respiratory infection. Research proved the microorganism to be a new member of the Coronavirus Family of viruses, an airborne virus, which quickly invaded bodies of human inhabitants where it swiftly replicated to spread across the world.

The rapid spread was accomplished by our modern system of global transportation systems. This organism was a Sars2 type virus and the disease was named Covid-19 for the year 2019 in which it was first recognized. In early 2020, Covid-19 produced a worldwide catastrophe, the largest pandemic in over a hundred years.

Populations in countries across the globe were unprepared since it had been a long time since a real and serious pandemic had emerged. This historical Covid-19 Pandemic would not end until widespread immunity was achieved, nor could it be controlled until more medicines for treatment emerged. Even the most advanced nations including the United States were unprepared. The health services were not prepared. The stockpiles of medicines and medical equipment in inventory were too minimal or ineffectual for such a catastrophe. The last time a pandemic of this type happened was a century ago, in 1918, and it erupted in a world where medical knowledge was much more primitive. Consequently, many millions of people died of the disease.

Because the previous 1918 Flu Pandemic occurred over a hundred years before 2020, the public had no real memory of what it might be like to live during this type of Pandemic. In the year 2020, the public generally believed that modern medicine had made such "plagues" a curse of centuries past.

Least of all, the public had no idea of the disruptions and radical social changes the Covid-19 Pandemic would bring about over time. Nor did the public recognize, as with past pandemics, it would permanently transform a world economy and a way of life. Instead, in 2020, most people simply thought about a time when everything in life would "return to normal." However, the "return to normal" would not happen because it could not happen. Living through the Covid-19 Pandemic would be shocking, severely disruptive and provoke permanent changes. Nevertheless, the Post Pandemic economy need not be a terrible one, in as much as the virus has created a re-constituted economy and innovation, and therefore a "New Normal." There would be no to return to the previous economy. Instead, the new economy will present abundant opportunities and therefore individual success requires planning for the future and making choices that are creative, informed and enlighten by research and inquiry. Good or bad, the past is the past.

## Impacts of Earlier Pandemics

In order to understand the future, it is well to first look into the past. Understanding how major pandemics have shaped past economies will provide insights into how the Covid-19 Pandemic will transform the economy.

Most everyone has heard of the "Black Death." It was a Pandemic, but few realize how it jump started economic develop. The Black Death ravaged Eurasia in 1346 before reaching Europe in 1347. It is estimated to have killed from 75 million to 200 million individuals in the Old World. In other words, the "Black Death" may have killed between a third of the population or perhaps as many and even 60% of the population of Europe in the years 1347 to 1353. It took almost two-hundred years for Europe to make up the loss in population.

The large decrease in population "accelerated" small economic changes that had begun to appear in land ownership and agricultural productivity. This change had slowly started earlier in the 14$^{th}$ Century, but after the Black Death it rapidly accelerated. These were rapid shifts which were recognizable as more and more demographic groups were increasingly involved.

After the Black Death subsided, a large portion of the labor force was dead, and the survivors were able to individually bargain for higher wages and better working conditions. The institution of serfdom, where labor was bonded to the land of specific landlords, was already declining at the time the Black Death struck and this decline was accelerated to the point of land-bonding disappearing in England and Western Europe. This inevitable economic change resulted in more workers moving from agricultural production to start small businesses or take jobs in the towns. Predictably, agriculture shifted to crops that required less labor. Large portions of agricultural land shifted from growing crops to grazing sheep and cattle. As economists say, "a change in Supply." Simultaneously, the increase in wages of the workers enabled them to buy the meat along with related products like wool and leather. As Economists say, "a change in Demand." The interactions of supply and demand are synergetic, and produce an observable time-valued outcome.

Due to the pandemic, the portion of land that was abandoned reverted to woodlands. As the trees matured, new opportunities arose for the business of producing timber products useful for the increasing size of the towns. This type of economic activity provided the basis for the modern market-based economy to emerge from towns that developed workplace specializations. The shortage of labor and consequent higher wages initiated an increased in Demand for replacing portions of human labor with technology, which promoted a culture of invention in Europe that would provide the basis for later technological progress. Combining these changes laid the foundation for economic progress in England and Western Europe. Southern Europe saw similar changes while the expanding markets in Western Europe created demand for the goods they imported from the Near East. The basis of the modern economy dates to the economic changes in Europe resulting from the Black Death Pandemic.

Later, in the 19th Century, recurrent epidemics of Cholera and Typhoid Fever accelerated the development of modern sewerage systems along with the development of municipal sanitation departments, and to finance these operations municipal bonds emerged as an investment instrument to fund their construction.

The global Russian Flu Pandemic of 1889 is another example of a pandemic that may have significantly impacted the economy. Although it was referred to as "The Russian Flu", recent speculation suggests it may have been a strain of Coronavirus that jumped from cattle to humans. It is estimated that the disease killed one million individuals worldwide. A complete picture of the 1889 Pandemic and its economic impact is difficult to determine due to insufficient information and other missing details.

Nevertheless, the 1889 Pandemic may have been a significant factor in creating the decade of excess in the United States known as the "Gay 1890's". However, its main value here is showing that global pandemics are not as rare as many believe.

## The 1918 Flu Pandemic

The last time a major global pandemic occurred in a modern economy was in 1918, and it was a global influenza pandemic, frequently referred to as the Flu Pandemic. The similarity to the Covid-19 Pandemic is its resemblance in economic impact, and therefore the 1918 Flu Pandemic will be discussed in more detail.

The 1918 Flu Pandemic came in three surges with the first in the Northern Hemisphere in the spring of 1918 and then, as with Covid-19, retreating in the summertime. The second wave of infection was far worse and initially began towards the end of August; this surge retreated near the end of 1918. A third and final wave appeared in the early months of winter in 1919.

Altogether, the 1918 Flu Pandemic infected about one third of the world population (33%, 500 million people) and 50 million are estimated to have died from it (90% survived). The total deaths were about three percent of the existing world population and 97% of population remained alive.

In 1918, the medical profession knew something of bacteria and the germ theory, but they did not have any direct understanding of viruses and there were no diagnostic tests. In fact, at the time, there still were some medical practitioners that had not yet accepted "Germ Theory" because they had been taught the false theory of "Spontaneous generation" (organisms magically arising from inanimate material).

Therefore, in the 1918 Flu Pandemic, there were no satisfactory pharmaceutical medications for influenza. There were no vaccines for viruses like the flu. The flu vaccines would not be developed until the mid-1930s, as a result of the research the 1918 Flu Pandemic had stimulated. Furthermore, these vaccines would not be widely available to the public until after World War II. The 1918 flu was a powerful and very deadly microorganism because it was new to the human population having made the jump from birds; it is believed most likely to have been from chickens.

Because humans did not have any immunity to the new virus it spread swiftly through the human population and approximately 10% of those infected died. Had the virus spread more slowly, the death rate of those infected would probably not have decreased, but a slower spread might have meant that more people would become aware of the spreading infection, and they might have considered the risks of getting the infection and therefore modified their behaviors.

However, in 1918, given the state of medical knowledge, there were few options for slowing the spread or trying to decrease infection. Even so, attempts at reducing its spread were tried using standard pandemic techniques including quarantines of those who were sick, the general wearing of face-masks, and increased hand washing; notice the same basic strategies were used in attempting to reduce the spread of Covid-19 a hundred years later.

A complicating factor in the 1918 Flu Pandemic was its occurrence during World War I when large numbers of people were moving around the planet and made it easy to spread the virus globally. Military personnel were often crowded together on troop ships and in barracks, ideal environments for spreading disease. The disease of 1918 became known at the time as "the Spanish Flu" because it was first reported in the press in Spain although it did not arise from Spain, and where it really came from no one knows. Given the history of flu pandemics since 1918, the suspicion today is that it originated in Asia but medical historians are still searching for its precise point of origin.

## Attempts at Mitigation

Making the public aware of the 1918 Flu Pandemic and understanding it seriousness was much more difficult than it is today. In 1918, households did not have televisions; they did not even have radios so there were no broadcast news networks.

Only by the late 1920's would radio broadcasting become commonplace. When it became available radio would prove to be the most common form of entertainment, but equally important it provided the public daily news broadcasts.

In 1918, quickly circulating *detailed information* across townships did not happen. For most of the population, only limited information was disbursed and announced infrequently. Signs and placards would be made and displayed where public traffic was usually encountered. Radio would have been vastly more helpful. However, radio was in the future, as broadcast technology did not exist in 1918.

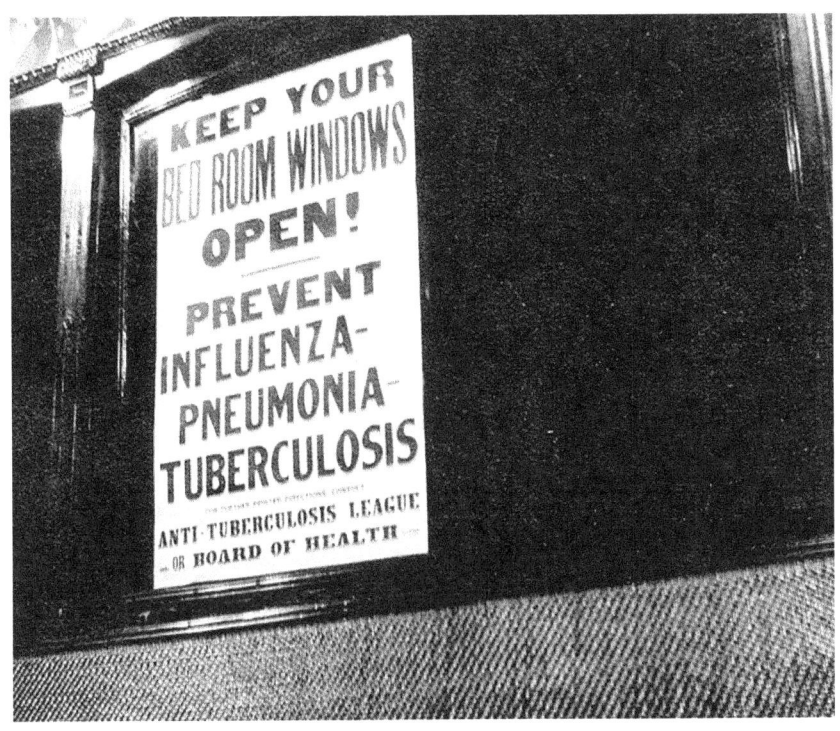

Credit: National Archives

In 1918, the means of public communication was largely limited to word of mouth, posters, telegraph and some newspapers. Many towns and small cities did not have a local newspaper. The larger cities did have daily and weekly newspapers, and articles on the 1918 Flu Pandemic quickly appeared in these publications. Mitigation techniques were communicated in the announcements and stories in newspapers and on flyers posted on public buildings.

The mitigation techniques prescribed were much the same as today. People were instructed to wear a face mask, to distance themselves from other people, to wash their hands often and to isolate if they experienced symptoms and felt ill.

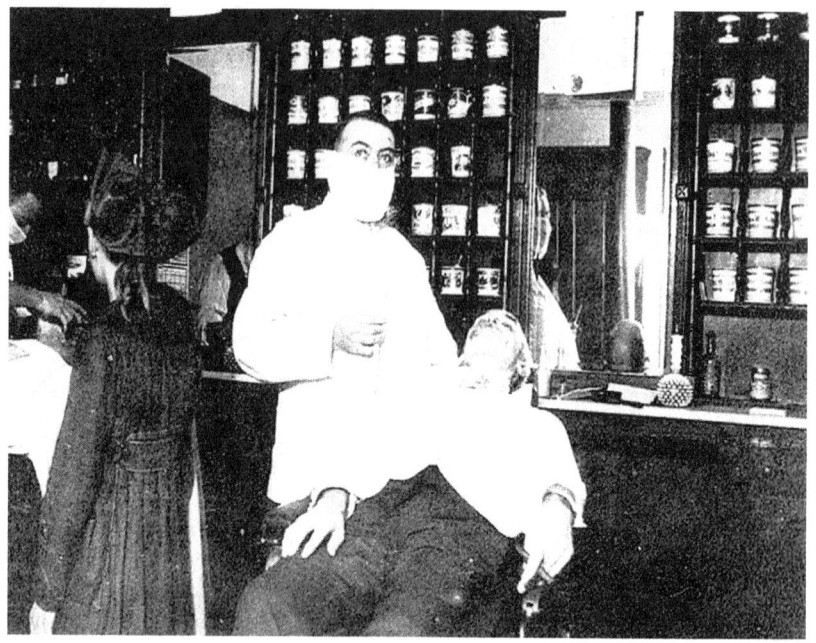

Credit: National Archives

Assemblies of large groups were frequently discouraged or prohibited. Businesses where entertainments and social gatherings took place were ordered closed. Many schools were closed for brief periods.

The wealthy citizens left the large cities where the virus was spreading and moved to their summer estates with private spacious grounds or simply bought homes elsewhere, far from the crowed cities. Those individuals without these options simply remained in their homes, and ventured out only for necessities such as food and work.

The demographic remaining behind in urban areas continued to follow the behavioral prescriptions of wearing masks, personal spacing and isolating as much as they individually thought necessary. These actions were carried out regularly throughout the course of the disease. Because affordable automobiles like the Model-T were still in short supply in cities, many depended on public transportation, which increased the spread of the disease just as it did with Covid-19 in major eastern American cities and in Europe where public transit is in common use.

## The Economy after the 1918 Flu Pandemic

By late 1920, the influenza had retreated as a result of the natural immunity that had built up in the people that survived while those most at risk had already died. The public gradually stopped wearing face masks, and returned to normal, but it was a "new normal". The short recession of 1920 that followed the end of WWI and the pandemic was quickly replaced by a booming economy.

The first major change in behavior was a significant increase in attention to personal hygiene to avoid infection by unseen "germs." Sales of personal hygiene products increased following the pandemic. This was accompanied by a huge desire to make daily life easier and more dynamic by purchasing not just automobiles, but also household appliances to render life simpler, all of this advanced the creating of the modern "consumer economy."

Although the buying of household appliances, and inexpensive automobiles dated to before the war and the 1918 Flu Pandemic, such a pattern of consumerism greatly accelerated after the crisis, as individuals put the bad memories behind them and embraced the modern Post-War world with enthusiasm. The percentage of the population using mass transit in America peaked in 1919, after which its long decline began as many Americans purchased automobiles and moved to the suburbs, accelerating a pre-war trend of moving out of crowded urban areas. The result was numerous new communities being created along major rail lines and highways where only farm land had existed previously.

The interest in moving factories out of urban areas also existed before the 1918 Flu Pandemic but this tendency accelerated as the population centers relocated out of urban areas. Business management also started providing cleaner facilities and healthier work environments, changes that were encouraged and promoted by public health departments. Another change, a likely result of the many deaths that survivors had witnessed during the Pandemic, was to seek more enjoyment out of life, the basis of what became known as the famous "roaring 20's lifestyle." The survivors did their best to forget the horror of the Pandemic.

As part of this trend for a more exhilarating life many Americans left rural areas for employment in the factories surrounding big cities. The boom in the consumer economy enabled this by creating numerous new jobs in factories.

At the same time, the demand for workers was boosted by a national xenophobia that emerged and resulted in the passing of numerous laws limiting emigration thereby reducing the supply of immigrant workers. This trend led to increased wages for existing workers. The acceleration of these barely observed pre-Pandemic trends combined with the new behavior patterns of the survivors of the 1918 Flu Pandemic, and created a new and divergent America in the 1920's. The magnitude of such changes was noted by Frederick Lewis Allen in his prescient book *Only Yesterday* although like most survivors he preferred to forget about the horrors of the Pandemic and never mentioned it in his book.

## Concluding Inference

The Pandemics of the Black Death in the 19th Century and the 1918 Flu in the early 20$^{th}$ Century are historic examples of how national economies are transformed by pandemics. The 1918 Flu Pandemic combined with the end of World War I and America's efforts in rebuilding Europe helped the spread of democratic governments to replace monarchies. Reactions to such upheavals created what historians came to regard as "the modern world."

# CHAPTER 3

## The 2020 Covid-19 Pandemic

At the start of the year 2020, the American public was feeling secure. Economic disruptions by Pandemics that had ravaged the world in the past were part of history. Diseases like Bird Flu, SARS, MERS, and Ebola created momentary worry, but these were quickly contained to limited regions, and diseases like West Nile Fever and Swine Flu turned out to be something much less than a pandemic. The public thought of these as non-events.

The last major global pandemic, the Flu of 1968, killed an estimated one to four million individuals worldwide, had passed quickly. Individuals, especially in western nations, felt so secure they stopped paying attention to warnings of possible pandemics. However, from here on, Covid-19 will be remembered for being responsible for massive disruptions and major changes in how we work and how we live. Covid-19 will eventually be remembered for how it created a new economy, post-Pandemic. In order to understand exactly how the new economy develops, we will examine and analyze the recent Covid-19 experience in all its manifestations.

## Review of the Covid-19 experience

In 2020, the primary individual that communicated information about Covid-19 to the White House and the public, and consistently appeared in the major news media, was Dr. Anthony Fauci. In 1984 he had been appointed director of the National Institute of Allergy and Infectious Diseases (NIAID), and he still held this position in 2020. The percentage of U.S. residents affected by the government's reactions, plans and public communications regarding Covid-19 was not large at first, but as the virus spread it eventually impact everyone in the nation.

The Covid-19 virus first emerged in China in late 2019. On New Year's Day, 2020, it was acknowledged worldwide that a new respiratory disease was infecting people in Wuhan, a major transportation hub in the interior of China. Until then few people in the West had heard of Wuhan. One month later, the virus was reported to have invaded Italy, initiating a flood of cases and then began spreading to other countries of Europe. By March, the virus was global. National borders were closed, air travel restricted, cruise ships quarantined, and the public placed into "lockdown", individuals restricted to their homes except for grocery shopping, critical outings or for necessary health care. The exceptions to a complete lockdown were the workers considered "essential workers" such as fireman, law enforcement, health care, and stores of similar critical functions such as grocery. Schools closed entirely. Offices closed, and many employees became "remote workers", using their home computers to work online. Restaurants closed services except for takeout and home delivery, and retail stores converted to online sales and curbside pickup. Global supply chains broke, resulting in stores running out of products for the first time in the memories of most individuals. The world changed overnight, shattering the feeling of security and comfort that had existed only days before.

With the advent of Covid-19, people learned that global pandemics were still possible in the modern world. We were told that even touching everyday objects could be dangerous and contact with other people was extremely risky. Simply breathing the air inside a building could now make you sick and might even kill you.

As the full impact of the Covid-19 virus was realized, acts of physical socialization quickly became another thing to avoid. The common handshake gesture upon first greeting someone was quickly eliminated along with other gestures such as the friendly pat on the back or placing an arm around someone's shoulders. Even standing closer than six feet apart was forbidden.

**This fear of the invisible microbe and the newfound awareness of vulnerability will not disappear entirely**

**after Covid-19 ceases to be a Pandemic and becomes endemic, because new behaviors that are enforced tend to persist and because of fear of new variants of the virus and their spread. Covid-19 destroyed the feeling of security and the idea that pandemics were only something you might read about in history books. Few people are risk takers, most are cautious avoiders and attitudes that have been developed during this Pandemic will not quickly go away.**

The public was told to "shelter at home," no physical socialization of any kind. Everyone was to wear masks whenever leaving the home for essential shopping for necessities or going to a pharmacy for medicine. Daily televised news about the virus became the norm. Television viewers were shown graphs of the theoretical **"Flattening of the Curve"**, which was used to defend the government orders of lockdowns.

The public thought of "Flattening the Curve" as a means to save lives. Actually, the shutting down of most of the economy was a measure undertaken to slow the spread of the virus, to allow time for ramping up the availability of medical supplies and equipment for the hospitals. The process of "Flattening the Curve" would push the timeline out; and the progress of some infections would be pushed to a later date, but this would not result in checking the virus, and it would certainly not end the viral infections. The endgame would only occur when an effective vaccine was developed or enough Americans were infected and developed natural immunity, thus conquering the virus.

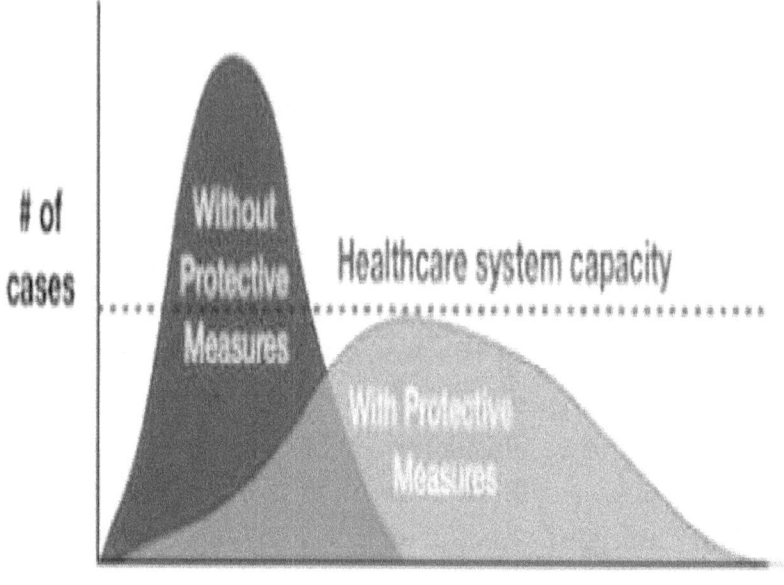

Adapted from CDC / The Economist

The first announcement of a two-week shutdown seemed reasonable to government officials, and most people accepted it and complied. After all, two weeks of doing nothing but staying at home was like a vacation break, a "staycation." It would not be unpleasant, and it would not be a huge dent in the economy.

However, when the two week "flattening" failed to have the expected impact, the decision was to extend the shutdown to thirty days hoping that would cause stricter changes in behavior as individuals began to fear for the future. Many people responded quickly by emptying of store shelves. Items such as toilet paper, paper towels, canned goods, some basic foods, and disinfectants were soon "out of stock". In this global economy, the supply chains had been made lean for decades because international firms aimed to minimize the cost of logistics. Such companies had spent years developing and implementing "lean supply chains" through business practices such as "just in time ordering" and "offshoring." These supply chains, however, could not handle the "demand shock" of store shelves so quickly emptied. This caused further panic buying of other products. It was only many weeks later that supply chains, some extending around the world, were able to deliver enough products so that merchants could partially restocked their barren shelves. **Note: it will take a long time for supply chains to fully adapt to the changes resulting from the Covid-19 Pandemic, and the process will continue throughout 2021 and into 2022**.

As the holiday of Easter approached in 2020, things would remain closed, shut down. People accepted this, but it also increased their fear. Places of spiritual worship remained closed, along with everything except for businesses deemed essential such as drugstores, supermarkets, and drive-through restaurants. All of this drove home how the Pandemic was viewed by government officials.

Because few people have training in statistical analysis and higher mathematics, the public continued to believe that the process of "Flattening the Curve" was something much more than just pushing the timeline out. Otherwise, they may have recognized that the area under the long flat curve that signaled rates of infection was likely to be nearly the same as the area under the steeper curve. This was true unless the virus mysteriously disappeared on its own or became less infectious.

**With minor exceptions, the long flat curve illustrates approximately the same number of people catching the virus, but over a longer period of time. Lacking scientific guidance on what was a completely new disease with a poorly understood transmission pattern, and most government officials lacking sufficient high-level knowledge in the subject of statistical analysis, the government officials simply continued to issue punishing shutdown orders to prolong the "flattening of the curve" month after month.**

Many state government authorities kept things shuttered for eight months or more by issuing fines for disobeying their orders. Fearful of a virus that they did not understand, and all the real implications of "flattening the curve" most of the public simply obeyed and hoped it would make the virus disappear.

This prolonged "flattening the curve" had three impacts: The first impact was a good one, allowing the medical community more time to acquire additional supplies and the resources needed to respond to the impact of this virus, especially in terms of personal protection equipment and hospital beds. It also gave the medical community time to learn how to treat the worst cases of Covid-19, and test therapeutic medications that might result in a reduction of the death rate.

However, the second impact of this protracted time of "flattening the curve" was a huge hit to the economy, which created millions of unemployed people, most suffering feelings of despondence while they "sheltered at home." They were unable to earn income or do the things they had previously enjoyed as their "normal lives."

**The third impact, and the one that is the focus of this book, is how widespread fear and the shutdowns created a new set of economic behaviors accelerating many existing economic tendencies while creating new trends. These behaviors will be reinforced as Covid-19 transitions from a pandemic status to an endemic status, and as new variants emerge. The process will cause new waves of infections throughout the world. This book explores the shape and structure of a new Post Pandemic Economy with an emphasis on the ramifications for the American economy.**

**Understanding the Post Pandemic Economy**The greatest impact of the virus on the economy will not be from the numbers of people that died, as woeful and such high mortality has been. **The greatest impact will be the transformations of daily life resulting from the population's reaction to the virus.** These will result in an evolution in consumer buying behavior, the emergence of remote work, the restructuring of supply chains to demographic shifts as individuals move out of urban areas to those with more space or lower populations.

As with past pandemics, the economic impact will be the legacy of the virus. The economic impact will be the result of a combination of the decisions by government officials, individual consumers, and business managements as they reacted to the crisis. As with past pandemics, many of these decisions will accelerate existing economic trends while creating new ones.

Businesses always look for ways that will avoid or at least reduce costly problems. Government officials need not attempt to be prescient and dictate the changes in production of products and services because the economy itself sends signals to business about what needs to be done. The totality of millions of businessmen and women reading these signals are far more knowledgeable than are government officials and their technical planners about what needs to be done and how the processes can be changed to improve production in the economy. This means government needs to be very cautious not to impede the implementation of cost effective and safe new ways to advance these processes of production and adapt to the "New Normal".

What should government "policy makers" do? What should they not do? The science of Economics tells us that government policy makers should not seek to be the solution for every problem but encourage the best solutions that arise in freely competitive marketplaces. The role of government is to provide channels for precise information on how the virus is transmitted and best avoided. Shutting down the economy for months at a time is a policy of *one-size-fits-all*, which cannot be a solution for hundreds of millions of people, nor should the government insist everyone adhere to the same adjustments or supposed solutions. Businesses have flexibility to utilize knowledge to and adapt their operations in order to optimize performance. The "wisdom of many people" as revealed in the marketplace makes free market economies capable of adjusting to shocks in the external environment. The one triggered by the Covid-19 virus is a prime example of this synergy.

When a government enforces broad, undifferentiated restrictions on businesses national commerce is reduced, shrinking both production and distribution of goods and services. The overall measure of economic production in a nation is called the Gross Domestic Product (GDP) of a country. The smaller the value of national GDP, the fewer goods and services are available for distribution, resulting in a reduction in the average standard of living.

In a nation with a market economy, these permutations will be determined as businesses react to the initial specific declines in sales of products and services as they adapt. Businesses thereby create the "New Normal." The short-term will have many permanent business casualties, 25% to 50% of businesses in any given community will fail and cease operations as a result of the Covid-19 shutdowns. However, as in all free market economies, new businesses with fresh business models will eventually rise to replace that vanished commerce.

## The Natural Reactions of a Market Economy

For many businesses, it is impossible to survive when government imposes severe restrictions on commerce for long periods. Certainly, this was true when many businesses were subject to government lockdowns and restrictions, in order to fight the spread of the virus. Yet, diverse medical experts supported such massive lockdowns designed to slow down the spread of Covid-19.

Nevertheless, the power of government is not the only force in a free market economy. Another powerful force is the flexibility and ingenuity with which free markets allow business leaders to adapt; the so-called "mother of invention." It is the nature of business in a free-market economy to seek ways to reshape their business models and to operate under the rules and restrictions that set by government. For example, when restaurants were forced to close their dining rooms, many started offering take-out, curbside pickup and even home delivery. After restrictions were loosened some establishments were then able to provide outside dining and thus partially satisfy their dine-in customers, albeit these are only temporary answers as restaurateurs attempted to hold on, waiting for long range solutions to appear or for governments to relax restrictions.

As the months rolled on under government mandated restrictions, some businesses were able to cover their expenses, while others without sufficient financial resources went out of business. For the survivors, pick-up, take-out and home delivery became a more commonly accepted practice. Consequently, new habits were formed by consumers and business managements, and many of these habits will persist into the Post Pandemic Economy. The jobs of waiters were replaced with employees handing take-out meals to customers curbside or delivery drivers.

The businesses, and their workers that adapted successfully survived and they will be part of the Post Pandemic Economy. That is the dynamic by which free markets operate. The survivors adapt and new businesses copy the successful business models. For example, at least one entrepreneur owning several restaurants immediately invested in a high-tech filtration system that uses ultraviolet light to dissemble viruses quickly and HVAC filtration rendering air clean and harmless. This adaption will make for a more pleasant and healthy dining experience and will become common in the Post Pandemic Economy.

Similarly, a number of shops in malls were able to survive by investing more in their online services. The Internet became their primary source of revenue and for many businesses a website was the only means of selling to customers. The government was responsible for the restrictions, but adroit business management was responsible for creative solutions to prevent bankruptcy.

For months, the public was essentially forced to forgo their previous shopping practices and adopt almost exclusively online shopping. Meanwhile, some local government-imposed crowd restrictions were partly relaxed and eventually allowed customers to return to stores.

The memories of both management and consumers will likely have an impact on how stores are designed in the Post Pandemic Economy. The new stores will be built around fewer walk-in customers, which will allow customers to individually socially-distance because stores will redesign how merchandise is displayed.

## Habits and the Obliging Free Market Economy

The many months of the forced Covid-Era experience of shopping online has formed new consumer habits of predominantly shopping online, even for customers that previously never did. These new practices will transfer a significant amount of consumer demand to online shopping. Readily apparent, the process grows as more and more suppliers compete in the online space for the sale of their products. Again, we see how reactions and adaptation to the experience of the Covid-19 Pandemic intensify earlier tendencies and establishes a dominant trend transferring this pattern into the Post Pandemic Economy, allowing for the confident forecasting of the future.

Suppliers of products and services support the permutations in buyers' demands, thus the overall relative costs of products can eventually decrease because some of the previous costs associated with physical space are no longer necessary. The overall fixed-costs of business are reduced. Meanwhile demand will continue to grow for delivery drivers and employees to serve the needs of curbside shoppers. In the free-market economy, businesses will increasingly deliver products to the customer.

When a crisis like Covid-19 unfolds, the long-term impact on a society and its economy are not random. Instead, change in and of itself interacts with existing developing economic trends to either accelerate or reverse them. To forecast the future, economists must be capable of assessing developing trends initiated by buyers and suppliers interacting with the alchemy of change. This is the dynamics of Supply and Demand over time.

During the pandemic, and in response to the government ordered lockdowns, consumers altered their shopping habits, work and lifestyle. Although these changes were thought to be temporary at first, many will become permanent in the "Beyond Covid Shock" economy. These changes have also served to accelerate several changes taking place in the existing economic landscape. The starting point for understanding the Great Economic Transition will be the impact of the trends accelerated by the virus lockdowns. In this book, the major economic motifs are identified, and we explore how diverse industries will be impacted in the emergent economy.

## Accelerating Economic Trends

In order to understand why the acceleration of the trends has a lasting impact it is necessary to know how innovations are adopted and are disseminated by an economy. Dr. Everett Rogers spent his academic career studying how innovation spreads through society. He published his work in a 2003 book *Diffusion of Innovation*. Dr. Rogers recognized that the speed which innovations diffused is a function of how the innovation is communicated over time through a social system. Each of the trends, as previously mentioned, represent innovation as to how work is performed or reflected in the lifestyle of individuals. The principles of innovation-diffusion teach us to determine how these trends will shape the Post Pandemic Economy.

Understanding how innovations diffuse throughout a society also provide us a method for analyzing how *Covid-19 lockdowns* have impact. The first step is to analyze the trends and the matrix of change. We ascertain how easy or difficult it will be for people to adopt these new trends. Dr. Rogers identified five characteristics of innovations that determined the likelihood of adoption. He called these characteristics:

1. *Relative Advantage*
2. *Compatibility*
3. *Complexity*
4. *Trialability*
5. *Observability*

The *Relative Advantage* of an innovation is essentially the benefits it provides over the traditional option that it replaces. One helpful example is the convenience of having a mobile phone to carry wherever you go. This is more beneficial to most individuals than the previous option of having a "landline" phone that was connected to a wall by wires and could only be used in a single room. The huge relative benefit ensures that mobile phones would be quickly adopted by a majority of the population whenever they were reasonably available.

*Compatibility* of an innovation, in the case of the mobile phone, was that it was entirely corresponding with the existing phone system after the cellphones reached a certain stage of technical maturity. This meant you could call anyone who had a phone, either a traditional one wired to the wall or a mobile phone.

*Complexity* is how difficult is it to learn how to use the new innovation. Although today the smart phones are very complex, the original mobile phones in the 20$^{th}$ Century were just as simple to use as the traditional phones. This made it very easy for individuals to learn how to operate them. It was only with the widespread adoption of the Internet that mobile phones started evolving into the very complex smart phones that we have today.

*Trialability* is often one of the big barriers to adopting an innovation, as individuals tend to be risk adverse about trying something new if they have to give up what they already have. Again, using the phone example, for mobile phones "Trialability" was easy because you did not need to give up your existing "landline" phone. You could keep and use both, and many individuals did for several years before abandoning their "landline" phones entirely, a process that is still ongoing even though 96% of Americans own a cell phone and an estimated 40% of households still had a "landline" phone in 2020.

*Observability* is the last characteristic of an innovation that impacts its adoption, and recognizes that the easier it is to see the benefits of an innovation, the more likely is it to be permanently adopted. With mobile phones the advantages of being able to quickly contact someone was very easy to observe. Although it still took about 25 years for mobile phones to be in widespread use that was a fairly short time in terms of the diffusion of a major innovation that transform lifestyles.

The ability of the different economic trends to satisfy all of these five characteristics of a successful innovation will determine how they will be accelerated by the Pandemic lockdowns which forced large segments of the public into what Dr. Rogers refers to as the *Innovation Decision Process*. The process consists of five steps:

1. *Knowledge*
2. *Persuasion*
3. *Decision*
4. *Implementation*
5. *Confirmation*

In the example of mobile phones, this was an individual process as each person first learned about these phones. Individuals were then persuaded to try these phones by friends, families and through advertising campaigns. As individuals tried the new type of phones, the benefits of mobile phone ownership were confirmed. This decision process will also be true of the acceleration of some of the other new economic trends. Virtual entertainment, online shopping, and automation existed before the Pandemic. However, as with other trends like remote work, online learning, or virtual meetings, the initial decision to use the innovation during the Pandemic restrictions and the benefits were so compelling that *confirmation* was reached.

Let us look at the five steps in terms of *remote work* and see how the process operates. In the case of *remote work*, many workers had only a vague notion that some individuals were able to work from home. In fact, only about 3% of workers were actual remote workers prior to the Pandemic.

When the state and local governments imposed lockdowns, the office employees of many types and particularly clerical workers not only became aware of remote work but also were required to become remote workers themselves. In this case, persuasion was simple, their supervisors directed them to "adopt the innovation" therefore the decision was made by their supervisors.

Implementation in this case was the company decision to use the innovation. The last step, *Confirmation* of the advantages, involves the remote workers on one side and management on the other. Most firms are still in processes of evaluation and experimentation.

Since the general benefits of remote work during the Pandemic lockdowns were clear to workers and to corporate management alike, the only other option was to close business down. In the beginning, the change from *work in office* to *work at home* was an easy decision for management to make because the office had to be closed, but business could continue with employees using the Internet and phones at home. However, the long-term *confirmations* of the benefits are being tracked and evaluated by corporate managements everywhere.

In terms of employees, some will find the change beneficial and will not only accept the innovation, but also demand it as the standard employment practice in the future. Others will not have liked it and want to reject it and these people will seek to return to the office if possible. Ultimately, the percentages in each category will determine the full extent of the impact on the economy in the "New Normal."

The authors of this book expect about 25% of the workforce will remain working remotely after the Covid-19 Pandemic. This major impact on the economy will be discussed in the next chapter. However, the simple magnitude of the overnight adoption of the innovation, from around 3% of the workforce to around 60%, will definitely leave its mark post-virus-shock as *The Great Economic Transition* evolves.

Few people actually have insight into the future because they have not had much knowledge of history, and most people are necessarily focused on their daily activities. Creators of powerful inventions that produce massive economic change with broad benefits are also few.

Moreover, even many of the Creators of inventions are not fully aware of the magnitude of their disruptions. The trends seen today are not entirely different from the past. For example, the company called Amazon began as an online bookseller, but continued to expand the types of products it sold. Today, Amazon appears to be taking over *all* the retail markets. Nevertheless, this is not really a new phenomenon because the concept actually began in the 19$^{th}$ century.

The company was called "Sears & Roebuck" and it operated largely without retail stores, but was a mail-order retailer. In 1893, Sears & Roebuck became the world's largest purveyor of merchandise by using paper catalogues for advertising, and customer ordering by mail, followed by shipping products to the buyers' addresses. Sears succumbed to the online competitor and ceased its business. However, Amazon is only different because it went entirely online. Today we have digital catalogues called websites. What was once paper is now digital imaging delivered over the internet to smart-phones and computer screens.

The Sears and Roebuck paper catalogue **offered more products than Amazon does, hundreds of thousands** of products of every conceivable type, including guns and prefab houses (all to be delivered to your chosen address).

## Concluding Inference

The evolutionary process impacts the economy in a number of ways. The economic landscape changes until it appears very different from the past. This will be one of the lasting legacies of the Covid-19 Pandemic that will shape the future economy.

As the economic landscape changes, the progression and direction of the change eventually becomes visible to everyone. The new images appear most everywhere, and the old fade from view. Some persons romanticize the past; while others are excited by what they come to believe is great progress. Those who see it as progress help to speed the process of change from the "Old Normal" to the "New Normal."

# CHAPTER 4

## Economic Trends & Covid

Just as with past Pandemics, the Covid-19 Pandemic will propel previously existing tendencies and economic trends, as well as develop new trends. Therefore, looking at trends and understanding how these develop and interact during the crisis should provide clear evidence of how people will live and work in the Post Pandemic era, and what precisely constitutes the Great Economy Transition

In response to the Covid-19 virus lockdowns of business, people needed to adapt their habits of work and lifestyle. Although these changes were thought to be temporary at first, many will be permanent in the Post Pandemic Economy. Our starting point for seeing by what means this takes place is to investigate how existing trends were accelerated by the virus via the implementation of restrictions on most economic and social activity, referred to as lockdowns. Eight major economic trends have been identified that were accelerated by Covid lockdowns and these will shape the Post Pandemic Economy. They are:

1. Remote Work
2. Robotics and Advanced Manufacturing
3. Virtual Meetings
4. Online Education
5. Virtual Entertainment
6. Online Retailing
7. Shortening of Supply Chains
8. Local Produce

In this chapter, we will discuss the impact of the Covid Shock on the economy as it pertains to *Remote Work, Virtual Meetings, Shortened Supply Chains, Agricultural Automation, and Robotics in Advanced Manufacturing*. The other developments in trends will be discussed in the following chapters.

## Remote Work

Remote work dates to the emergence of the Internet in the mid-1990s. In the last two decades, the number of individuals working remotely has been increasing and estimated at around 4% of the workforce prior to the virus striking. Literally overnight, the number increased to 40% and then estimated to be closer to 50% of the workforce. This huge increase has changed the image of remote work from being the domain of a handful of tech savvy workers to mainstream. Managers originally were often fearful that their employees working from home would have limited productivity. However, the great majority have actually seen productivity at the same level or even increase. This is due to:

1. The workers reduced stress of not having to spend an hour or more commuting to an office.
2. The workers being able to focus on tasks without the usual office distractions.

Managers also began recognizing:

1. Remote work eliminates the need for having expensive offices in prestigious locations.
2. Remote working eliminates the cost of keeping those offices operating.

Management experts estimate that a business will save $11,000 to $12,000 per worker per year by allowing them to work from home. The savings result from the reduction in the amount of office space needed, the cost of utilities and the custodial services required to maintain the office space. These savings will be even larger for business located in urban areas with premium prices for office space. This is a substantial financial incentive for management to switch to remote work platforms.

Workers have found working from home is much less stressful than going into the office. Instead of having to eat a quick breakfast and then rush out the door for a harried commute, they simply have to go to their home desk and turn on the computer. Since their productivity is measured by the work performed and not the hours spent in a cubical, they are free to take a break when they wish, spend a few moments with their kids, or walk their dog. These relaxing activities allow them to work at peak performance when they return to their work tasks. The workers also find they are saving thousands of dollars per year by not commuting or having to dress for the office. The result is that over three quarters of those working from home want to continue to do so after the Pandemic crisis recedes. Given the huge savings and gains in productivity that businesses have experienced, executive management will likely take advantage of furthering the gains by allowing them to do so.

Like virtual meetings, the accelerated trend of working from home has major economic consequences.

- The urban office building, an innovation of the late 19$^{th}$ Century, and persisted throughout the 20$^{th}$ Century and into the early 21$^{st}$. However, urban office structures will fall out of favor with managers of many businesses. Already several businesses have started reducing the amount of office space they are renting in urban areas. This will impact not only the urban market for commercial offices but also the environment of the urban economies that emerged in the last 150 years because there will be far less need to support giant office structures.

- Likewise, there will be less need for the mass transit systems used to reach restaurants and coffee shops. There will be less need for transportation of workers that provided maintenance and support for large urban office buildings. Already city officials are seeing the potential impact and downward pressure on taxes and are pressuring businesses to return workers to the office building for the "civic good" However, given the huge savings and productivity gains from remote work, it will be a very hard sell.

## A look inside the office buildings

As more individuals work remotely, the need for enormous and expensive high-rise office buildings will definitely decline. The government lockdowns forced a large number of previous office workers to "shelter-at-home" during the early phases of the Pandemic. Business management could not refuse, and management had to tell the workers to "work from home." Business leaders and most employees thought the "shelter-at-home" would be for a brief time and then it would be back to the offices for everyone. Although originally the shelter-at-home order was to be a couple of weeks, this order was extended again and again as the COVID-19 infection rate remained high. Meanwhile, management found that productivity and worker satisfaction increased when they were working from home. As a result, companies quickly assessed the potential of having the office workers continue working at home for an extended period, using the Internet communication. Thousands of offices in high-rise buildings remained vacant as the workers are working "at home." It is important to recognize that after digital voice, fax, text and video communications became commonplace most office workers actually did not need to be collected and corralled into a large multistory building in order to accomplish ordinary daily tasks:

1. There is no need to leave one office to communicate with someone in another office.

2. There is no need to carry a paper document from one office to another office on another floor of the huge building.

3. Full time, trained and experienced office employees do not need the physical presence of supervisors to look over their shoulders.

Therefore, most office workers actually did not need to be clustered in offices and cubicles in large buildings. Personal computers and Internet have been widely available for years. Most workers can accomplish all their assigned tasks while they reside in their own homes or perhaps elsewhere if they desire.

Previously, it was inertia that prevented businesses from taking full advantage of the flexibility, efficiency and cost savings the technology offered. The Covid-19 lockdowns changed that by forcing business to use the new technology to its fullest extent for remote work.

The impact of having most employees performing their tasks as "remote workers" will be far reaching. This will be perhaps the most important economic impact arising from the Covid-19 Pandemic. Indeed, office rents have already started falling in large cities.

The decreasing demand for office space will likely result in some of the high-rise office buildings eventually being retrofitted for entirely different purposes than they were originally intended. One might imagine a building with many different restaurants, various salons and other activities.

Likewise, the competition will increase between suppliers of office and conference areas on a rent by the day basis or even by the hour for meetings. Such daily or hourly rental prices are likely to decline significantly.

For example, during the Pandemic the Nike Corporation transitioned its office workers to become remote workers due to the lockdown. Subsequently, in January 2021 Nike vacated office buildings it had rented in Portland. The move accounted for about 279,000 square feet of vacant office space.

The lack of demand for office space may result in other office buildings being converted into residential space for those individuals who want to live in urban centers. Other benefits will be in the reduction of commuting and traffic which were previously associated with peak travel hours. In addition, there may be less air pollution in the less congested post-viral urban centers. All of this will also reduce the risk of new viruses in urban areas. Nevertheless, there will still be some constraints remaining in the ability to provide flexibility throughout a viral outbreak. For example, in highrise buildings, irrespective of purposing, the elevators cannot provide sufficient social-distancing potential during a viral outbreak. Adding new and larger elevator shafts is often not an option.

Credit: Pexel Samuel Walker

As is always the case with privately run efficient free markets, as compared to government owned and planned production and distribution, some of these repurposing attempts for the existing high-rise will fail as others become successful, which produces the best solutions. Nevertheless, the landscapes of cities will change in ways that were previously unimagined and otherwise impossible for government planning to be efficient.

**Eventually, even with repurposing of traditional office "skyscrapers," a number of the skyscrapers will become less useful, and these giant edifices will become the *fossils of concrete and glass dinosaurs* in the Post Covid Shock Economy.**

## Robotics and Advanced Manufacturing

Many manufacturing activities involve the interaction and coordination of workers that are physically present in buildings. These activities require a business place of operation. Some degree of safety equipment, distancing and barriers are possible, but are not desirable as permanent design. New methods will probably involve more automation, robotics, and greater employment of Artificial Intelligence (AI). The acceptance and conversion to the employment of new technology like 3D Printing and adaptive manufacturing will be accelerated in the Post Pandemic Economy.

As early as May 2020, a survey of 681 employers found that 74% had made adjustment to the work environments for employees returning to job sites. These were commonly the addition of barriers, safety equipment, distancing protocols, and adjustments to their use of automation. Nevertheless, half of their full-time employees were working remotely or from home.

**Following the Covid Shock, we can expect management to begin to significantly plan for the increased adoption of robotics and AI solutions in factories. The International Federation of Robotics reported that the cost of robots has decreased and continues to decrease enabling wider adoption.**

Already South Korea has seven robots per 100 workers, and one third of all robots are in China. Before the pandemic, predictions of massive job losses were the focus of topics on Robotics and AI. Throughout the pandemic, massive job losses occurred because of the lockdown imposed by government, but not because of automation.

The discussions now focus on how automation can accelerate recovery and protect from possible future economic downturns as a result of Pandemics or other crises. Considerable thought will be devoted to the application of the new manufacturing technology. Some of the displaced factory workers will be able to find employment in the industry producing the automation equipment. However, others will have a hard time gaining new skills. The people that realize what is happening in the Post Covid Shock Economy will be better prepared for success in readying themselves for new employment by studying the opportunities before their industry transitions to automation. Workers' job planning is discussed and outlined in Chapter 10 of this book.

Automation will also shorten supply chains as the cost of labor becomes a less important factor in locating production facilities. This will encourage production facilities to be placed closer to the demand for the product, thereby shortening the supply chains.

Ingenuity and thoughtful reactions to the Pandemic have already sponsored many changes in workers' jobs or in some cases eliminated the jobs entirely. For example, the recycling industry quickly reacted to the possibility of the spread of virus by human handling of the plastic and cardboard waste. One of the proposed solutions was robotics, and the idea quickly caught on. AI Robots capable of doing the pickup and sorting of materials were already being produced, but the reaction of recyclers was to order many more. The job of what previously was called the "Trash Man" (now more often called Waste Collector) fades into history as AI Robotics takes over.

The acceleration in substitution of AI Robotics for human workers in manufacturing will continue to increase in many areas of production. Although jobs will be lost to automation new jobs will be created to build and service the robots that replaced those workers. These substitutions will become a significant part of the new Post Covid Shock economy.

Recently, in San Diego, California, there are sewage-testing robots involved in the processing of wastewater. Robots test for viruses, and can predict where new outbreaks of viruses may take place.

Robotics will not only be involved in processing and work activity, but also increasingly be substituted for human interaction directly with the consumer. These machines may not look like humanoid, but more like the ATM machines that substitute for retail bank clerks. This increasing substitution of machines for human contact has been going on for decades, but the trend will accelerate and characterize one of the most impactful differences between Post-Covid life and the "Old Normal."

Some people are wondering about their occupational viability in face of the evidence of advancing robotics in their industry. "Will Robots replace you and takeover your occupation?" Robotics has already replaced some people because it can frequently do a better job and at less expense to the business, and eventually a relative lower unit price to the customer. This process will accelerate in the "New Normal" of the Great Economic Transition.

There is a solid economic reason why robots will increasingly replace human workers. People are biological entities that continually require more resources per day than a computerized mechanical entity. Humans can be distracted and make a mistake. Robots do not. Humans can become tired and lose energy, slowing down their work. Robots do not.

Furthermore, humans require psychological and cultural management, but robots do not. Psychological and cultural management are time consuming activity that requires extensive knowledge, sound processes of management, and this adds to overall expenses in doing business. You can understand why business management wants to replace human workers. People involve additional expenses that increase the cost of doing business.

Currently, the application of robotics is progressing within the simpler, repetitive, routine types of work. For example, kiosks are cropping up in many places where before only humans interacted. Repetitive tasks are another example especially in storage facilities such as stacking and retrieval of materials from shelves. These are tasks easily accomplished by robotics.

This is only the beginning. We will soon see the pace pick up. In some fast-food-restaurants, kiosks are already taking food and beverage orders. In addition, there are other robots which can be programmed to deliver these orders to your restaurant table or service counter. There is no need for human waiters and therefore no need for the waiter's gratuity. Nevertheless, there will probably be some sort of "service charge" added to the price of your food order.

## Conclusion

There will be far less opportunity for contact with human beings. Many of the new machines will be "smart" in the sense that we now use smart electronic assistants, but the problem is that living in the Post Pandemic "New Normal" will mean that we have far fewer material encounters with other people in the work areas and in non-work environments as well. Currently, the exploration of consequences of this major change for human beings can be considered at an early stage of scientific investigation.

What will it mean for humanity in general? Will people everywhere attempt to "socialize" emotionally with these machines? Today, most people are already accustomed to computer interactions and using "smart assistants." Everyone is familiar with the imaginative spectacles in hundreds of cinematic films. What was once imaginative is fast becoming a new reality. How does this change human interaction, society, and the economies of the world?

What will we learn about the impact on humans that have fewer and fewer opportunities for interaction with other people? This question will be part of scientific studies in Psychology, Sociology, Social Anthropology, and the Humanities in general and throughout the "New Normal" of the Post Pandemic Economy, the new adventure of our era.

# CHAPTER 5

## Lifestyles after the Covid Shock

For many people, most of the year 2020 was spent in their homes and apartments. Leaving home, whether for work, dining or entertainment was not an option because state governors, city mayors and city councils required that only "essential" trips to supermarkets or for exercise outdoors were allowed, but people going outside were to be no less that six feet away from each other. Often due to capacity limits imposed by the governing authorities, there were long lines outside of supermarkets or the big-box retail outlets. Widespread "Lockdown Restrictions" were imposed upon all such activities in order to delay and thereby slow the spread of Covid-19. These long lines lasted for many weeks all through the first wave of the Pandemic. Summer came, and restrictions continued in force for business lockdowns and any form of social gatherings throughout the summer of 2020.

Later, in the autumn, the more restrictive lockdown orders were imposed on many regions of the nation. These restrictions by government authorities continued and were even expanded to most regions when the Winter Wave of Covid increased. The restrictions changed individuals' habits, **and some of the people who are more risk adverse will continue to wear masks and socially distance even after the enforcement by regulation and mandates have ended.**

## The New Normal

A great deal changed during the Covid-19 Pandemic. The people around you altered their behaviors, daily life activities were revised, and our view of the world was never again to be the same. You have probably changed in ways that you never imagined. Before Covid-19, most people had a vast array of splendid activities, live-events, theatrical performances, festivals and more they could attend without fear. Amusement parks, local zoos and libraries were open as were recreational facilities, cafes, bars and restaurants. Whole communities were often gathered in various venues. Opportunities for physical socialization abounded.

With the advent of the Covid-19 Pandemic, lives instantly became more isolated. Most people still felt the need for communing with others, but the thought of catching potentially deadly Covid-19 from mingling and socializing induced a high level of fear. People obeyed the official regulations and sheltered alone or they lived with only a few family members in the same household. Friends and acquaintances were often shut out, and people remained alone or in small groups. People missed seeing their friends, sharing their lives and "hanging out". At first, the public thought this isolation and austerity was only temporary, but after more than half the year elapsed, people began to wonder if society would ever be the same again. Then the Winter Wave of the Pandemic struck in the autumn season and every month thereafter for the entire year. This further strengthened most people's suspicion that their previously normal daily lives would not return. This view is supported by scientists who now believe that Covid-19 will be endemic with new variants causing new waves periodically similar to the flu virus although perhaps at a more serious level.

Looking at a few more of the specific activities, facilities and institutions, we can see how they fared, and how they changed. This evolution was the push toward the "New Normal" in the Post Pandemic era.

## Health Care

For quite some time, the technology to conduct a variety of doctor visits by Internet video communication existed, but used minimally. Before Covid-19, a doctor's appointment by Internet video was not broadly available and Medicare would not pay for it. In some states, the practice was not permitted. This changed in 2020. Many doctors in order to protect their patients from the spread of the virus began using live-video by Internet as a necessity. Soon the physicians were finding that it provided many other advantages. It is likely that many more physicians will adopt it as a standard in their practices. Most patients prefer it because it saves them travel to an office and sitting in a "waiting room."

**The implications of remote medicine are enormous. With a widely available remote medicine system, people will be able to locate and discuss their health problems with specialists from other towns and cities. Patients will be able to find the best physicians for their needs. Medical specialists will be able to expand their practices beyond their physical location, without having to move to other locations.** With remote medicine, people have a greater opportunity to receive the type of health care they desire. Furthermore, like everything else, the technology will improve as innovative new software and delivery systems develop to meet the expanding remote practices. It will help modernize health care in many regions of the nation.

# Online Shopping

An activity that existed since the emergence of the Internet in the 1990 is online retailing. However, the lockdowns and restrictions imposed by the Pandemic greatly accelerated online retailing as mentioned earlier. In 2019, an estimated 11% of retail sales were online. With the Covid-19 lockdowns, the forced closing of stores and the long-lines for shopping created at the few stores permitted to be open, online shopping greatly increased. In 2020, the percentage of online retail sales doubled. For many customers online was the only option to buy what they needed, especially those in high-risk groups. The result was a huge increase in online shopping with both home delivery and curbside pick-up offered. Many consumers made purchases online for the first time, especially for basic needed items like groceries. Others ordered complete meals online for pick up or delivery for the first time. Having experienced the ease of shopping online many people will continue to do much of their shopping online after the Covid crisis is over. **The trend away from physical retailing was accelerated by the Pandemic, changing forever the retail industry, and is discussed in more detail in Chapter 7.**

## Virtual Entertainment

Another trend that existed before the Covid-19 virus was the emergence of virtual entertainment in the form of webcams, VR tours and virtual worlds. Adoptions of all three have significantly expanded since the virus lockdowns. Home computer screens were substituted for movie theaters and live performance stages, popular forms of entertainment across generations. Many people, bored by lockdowns, ventured into virtual worlds like "War of Warcraft" to explore and take part in these simulations of reality or to explore lifelike renderings of make-believe. **Expectations are that membership in the online virtual worlds will increase by 10% per year following the Pandemic.**

National parks, museums, zoos and similar attractions expanded existing webcams and expanded their virtual offerings to make them available to those stuck at home by the lockdowns. Some of these online activities will prove to be revenue enhancement derived from the marketing influence, and thereby increase paid live-attendance in the Post Pandemic Economy.

## Movie theaters and Video

Movie theaters were especially hard hit by the Pandemic. Before Covid-19, the movie theaters had survived stiff competition from introduction of television, cable programming and streaming movies over the Internet. Movie theaters had been an enduring feature of both small towns and big cities everywhere. The release of a major new film at the local theater was frequently an exciting event. People looked forward to "going to the movies."

However, audience attendance was shrinking even before the Pandemic struck, because of both the increasing recent affordability of large screen televisions in the home, an abundance of movie streaming services, and the increased theater ticket prices. As a result, some theater chains were already having difficulty. After state and local governments, in response to the Covid-19 virus, ordered movie theaters to shut down there were no earnings possible. After months of being closed or under capacity reductions, what may have been difficult before the government restrictions became financially frightening, and an impossible situation for some theater owners.

Many individuals, unable to go to movie theaters, started "watch parties" with their friends to share the experience on their big screen home TVs while still social distancing at home. **This lifestyle trend will have many implications for the entertainment industry.** The primary reason for having previously survived during rapid social change was that some types of filmed performances are more enjoyable when experienced sitting alongside of other people in an auditorium. For example, the audience reacts as they see a feature length comedy. Some people burst out laughing at a comedic scene, which induces others to laugh along, and this enhances the emotional experience. The fact that most of the large audience are strangers to each other but have the same reactions to the movie reinforces a comfortable sense of sharing and comradery. Movie theaters are a social space, like a live stage performance, but with other features not possible in live performance.

**"Social distancing" became a common phrase under the orders of government officials. Nevertheless, social distancing is an oxymoron. Human nature will continue to seek socialization in the "New Normal" of the Beyond Covid Shock era. As we are seeing, things will never be the same, but people in the Post Pandemic Economy will make choices from the array of changes provided in the economy by the competitive motivation in the free market system.**

Human beings, and even many social animals, seek social spaces because shared experiences can be deeply satisfying. It is both an instinctual and a learned desire to group together. Sitting at home alone and watching a motion picture cannot provide that same emotional experience, no matter how large the home screen nor the matter the quality of your surround-sound system. The movie theater is a social space for shared experience. The films provide large facial close-ups of the actors, which cannot be seen in a live theater performance. Films utilize cinematic camera tricks, computerized imagery and 3D effects that enhance realism and fantasy alike. Therefore, movie theaters have remained a valued addition to the entertainment industry.

During the lockdowns, a few theater owners reintroduced the Drive-In Theater. The Drive-In was highly popular in the 1950s and though the 1960s, but over time the alternative value of land-use outstripped the revenues from operating a Drive-In theater. Nevertheless, a reintroduction was a partial and temporary solution for a few theater owners. Again, we see that flexibility and adaptation are key business management tools in a market economy.

The older adults, the senior segment of the movie going audience exhibit the highest level of risk aversion. The young are not as risk adverse as older adults. The young are biologically driven to be adventurous and to seek excitement and pleasurable experiences. It is no accident that in the Pre-Covid era the largest segment of cinema audience was the young adults. Specifically, 25-39 year-olds were the largest movie-going demographic. This segment of the public has dictated the type of films produced. Furthermore, it is this demographic that most desire the experience of so-called "blockbuster" movies. It is well known that there are no new stories yet untold, there is no new plot yet to discover. The fiction writers of novels and screenplays can only nuance and retell the stories in a new mix of imagery and actors.

The film producers and directors attempt to follow audience demands as much as possible. The theater environment is the only venue for delivering the impressive spectacles that appeal to the young adult demographic. There is no reason to expect that this segment of the public will change their behavior and preferences in the Post Covid Shock Economy.

By late summer of 2020 state government restrictions on movie theaters were partially eased, but this was insufficient to save many theaters. New York was the key to halting the severe financial bleeding of exhibitor's profits. In mid-October, the Global Cinema Federation sent a letter to Governor Mario Cuomo pleading with the governor to release a plan that would allow theaters in counties with low incidence of new infections to open their cinemas. Interesting was the fact that there had been no known Covid-19 outbreaks linked to theaters located in the United States or anywhere in the world. Furthermore, industry specialists explained why without New York opening its theaters, the movie industry could not return to any level of profitability. New York was one of the largest film markets in the world. Distribution of new films begins with New York, which provides important marketing for the other areas of distribution.

In late autumn, when the new Winter Wave of the Pandemic began to take hold, the theaters were once again shut down. As the most profitable markets remained shuttered, the industry's box office receipts were expected to be down 76% by the end of 2020 even before the new Winter Wave of the Pandemic struck. With movie theaters completely shut down a second time, viewers once again turned to streaming services for their entertainment, selecting movies and serials to watch. "Watch parties" in which groups of individuals gathered on social media to watch movies, concerts and shows became common. New habits were created that will persist into the Post Pandemic Economy. The recent decision by Warner Brothers to send all new movies direct to streaming media will reinforce the social trend towards streaming media and provide additional pressure on movie theaters.

## Live theatre

Live theatrical performances and concerts suffered many of the same problems as the movie theaters. Performances beginning in the March of 2020 and continuing through the rest of the year into next were postponed. Initially, producers rescheduled looking toward the fall or holiday season, and then announcing that performances would not happen until sometime in the next year, perhaps not until the summer of 2021 or later. Musicians, dancers, actors and all the supporting workers were faced with a year or more of unemployment. The famous venues for live performances of all types were closed and locked up for a year or more. Some of these went to live-streaming and it will be only a matter of time before they make the transition to VR technology, allowing individuals to watch performances from home in multi-dimensional realism.

**Post Covid Shock, the change for movie theaters will be fewer venues in the "New Normal."** In addition to the theater owners' financial losses throughout the Covid Pandemic, a portion of the public will continue to avoid packed theaters for an extended time period because the new habit has been ingrained in certain segments of the public much like other new habits gained during the Covid-19 Pandemic. **Movie theaters will not totally disappear, live performance venues will not disappear, but there will be fewer film and live theaters surviving for the Post Covid Shock era, and somewhat smaller audiences.** Movie theaters have serious work to do reinventing their business models in the Post Covid Shock Economy.

## Online learning

Education was another part of an individual's lifestyle that changed greatly because of the Pandemic. Government reactions to Covid-19 Pandemic quickly expanded the application of the online learning education models. Students at all levels were switched overnight to online learning. Online education also dates to the emergence of the Internet. In 2019, approximately 15% of college students in the United States took all their classes online while approximately 48% had taken at least one online class. In terms of K-12 the numbers were much smaller with only about 5% of students in the United States taking online classes, generally those who were intentionally being home schooled. As a result of the Covid-19 lockdowns, education changed virtually overnight with the vast majority of the 48 million K-12 students going online for their schooling.

Unfortunately, the rapid movement online created major problems with the quality of education falling as millions of teachers who were never trained in online education took their classes online using Zoom and other video conferencing technology. Not being trained in online instruction they taught the students using the only techniques they knew, which were designed for face-to-face instruction. This was not surprising to experts in online learning like the authors, who pioneered online learning in the 1990's. Teaching online requires a different approach and pedagogical method than face-to-face instruction. A quality online course often takes months to design and it was fool hardy to think that instructors with no online experience or training could move their classes online in only a matter of days. It should be no surprise that the forced overnight shift to online learning produced dismal results and a lost year of learning for most students.

Sadly, this failure to provide quality online classes will leave many with the impression that online learning is a poor substitute for face-to-face learning where assessments consistently show students in a quality online class can often outperform those in face-to-face classes. This is especially true in high school and college level classes. Still this rapid movement online will accelerate the move towards online learning. Those students fortunate enough to be in quality online courses designed by online qualified faculty will see the benefits and flexibility it allows. **As such, the Post Pandemic Economy will likely see online learning to continue expanding among high school and college students.**

For the college aged students, taking courses online was already a common option or experience. Adult students can do well in online learning, assuming that the professor is good at using the online software tools and pedagogy for teaching and guiding adult students. Online programs that are delivered asynchronously provide time and space flexibility for students. Asynchronous discussions between students can be valuable and held to high standards. The questions regarding needs for live synchronous physical socialization largely depends on the degree of socialization in the individual's personal environment and personal preference. Therefore, Post Pandemic, it is likely to remain the same for many adult students.

Most high school students were especially challenged by learning programs placed totally online during the Pandemic. These social shortcomings will still exist in the Beyond Covid Shock era. The teenage years require significant social interaction that cannot be provided by simply using Zoom or any other Internet on-screen visual program. **High School in the United States is not merely a learning activity; it is also a social activity, with sports having a significant role in most school districts. For this reason, it is unlikely that the average school district will invest the resources to compete with the existing vir-**

tual high schools. Younger children were even more challenged by totally online distanced learning programs as has been evident from the Covid lockdowns. As parents who have home schooled their children know, it is necessary to provide social interaction in the form of sports and other social activities. The result will be that most school districts will abandon online learning and return to face-to-face classes as soon as they are allowed to do so.

In the course of the Covid-19 Pandemic, the "shelter at home" experience included parents as well as their children, and many of the parents observed the effects of their children's experiences with the online learning. Schools were closed, and many teachers were teaching "online distance courses." Students were home, usually with a parent close by. As the students sat behind their computer screens, the parents if they wished could also view the online lesson and hear everything the teacher said. Parents for the first time saw what was being taught to their children. Rather than school being a type of "black box" were kids were sent for the day to learn, the "at home online" experience allowed the parents to secretly become viewers of the learning process. **This prolonged exposure to their child's online instruction made parents more aware of the challenges of instructing children on the Internet. Furthermore, these parents were now more aware of what was being taught. As a result, this experience is likely to change attitudes toward public school-**

ing. **In response some parents will seek changes to what is taught in public schools while others, will seek home schooling alternatives that will provide the education outcomes that parents are seeking**. The expansion of remote work will also facilitate this change, as more parents will be at home to supervise and support their children learning at home.

It is also likely that some sort of hybrid design combining some in-person school based social activities with home online learning will become an option at the more forward-looking school systems seeking to prepare their students for the digital future.

Public education in the Post Pandemic era will be greatly impacted by the experience of online learning during the Pandemic. School districts will need to regain parents' trust and approval following the failure of remote learning. The opportunity for competition by private schools is likely to enlarge as active parents demand the environment for school choice. Together these factors will provide impetus and endorsement of more positive educational experiences.

**The Pandemic is also likely to influence education in another way and that is in terms of career choices. More high school graduates will likely decide to enter the trades. They have seen the effects of college graduates unable to earn the expected higher incomes and they have seen others losing their jobs during the Pandemic. The next group of high school grads already know of many college graduates that**

**struggle financially because of borrowing huge debt to pay the college and university expenses. However, they are also seeing the demand for workers in the trades. When they see the job security, income and benefits common to carpenters, electricians, plumbers, and other trades have been outpacing most of the traditional college graduates, many of the high school graduates will opt for these trades**. There will also be an increased demand for these jobs as remote works leave cities and buy homes in rural and the expanded suburban areas. Spending a larger portion of their life at home means they will spend the money, previously used for commuting, on improving their home environment. This will definitely create a greater demand for individuals with the skills to do home remodeling and upgrades.

There is also likely to be an accompanying change in the behavior of employers. Corporate managements may well realize that their policy of hiring only college graduates was not the best practice because many of those recruits lacked important skills and knowledge the companies needed, and the new hires had to be trained by the company. These companies will hire high school graduates instead, and train them specifically in the skills and knowledge needed in their industries. Unions may also gain following the Pandemic and expand their traditional role in providing workers with security and training. Both of these actions will reverse the concept that everyone needs a college degree to obtain a "good job" that pays well. This reality will reverse the previous trend that began in the in the USA and elsewhere during the 1960s. Few parents of that time had been college graduates with bachelor's degrees or higher professional degrees, but they shared the idea that their children must go to college and learn more. In 1965, the percentage of Americans with a bachelor college degree was 9 percent, but over the years, this figure climbed to an astonishing 36 percent. This 400% increase was not warranted as many of these college graduates could not find employment that drew upon their college studies. Moreover, many graduates still lacked the basic, communication and occupational skills needed by many employers.

**Education like other aspects of the Economy will not be the same. Superficially, schools will reopen, and students will return, but the change of lifestyles by their parents will slowly ripple through education.** Many parents working from home will want their kids to be prepared for the "New Normal" and will look for high quality but lower cost online learner options. Others will let their children return but will demand more training in technology to prepare them for the new Post Pandemic experience. Many high school students along with college students will change their career goals in response to the Pandemic, seeking more secure options. Many will also seek careers that will allow them to take control of their future instead of putting it in the hands of employers. **Unemployed because of structural changes in the economy many**

workers will return to schools in order to train for new careers. Administrators of Education at all levels will need to recognize, understand, and adapt to these changes if they wish to contribute to the new Beyond Covid Shock Economy and be successful.

## Home Sweet Home

One major feature of the Beyond Covid Shock Economy will be the renewed emphasis on family and the home in the post-Pandemic period. The shutdowns of the economy were severe, the fear traumatic, and home appeared to be the safe place. Because so many people spent most of the year 2020 at home, it became the focal point of their life. The experience caused people to view their homes differently. Instead of simply being a place to rest between work, school and other activities it became the center of their world during the Pandemic. As one television commercial put it, "Home is everything."

An important motivation for changes in the types and locations of homes demanded involved the move towards remote work that accelerated during the Pandemic. This previously unplanned experience proved that remote work done in the home was productive and less costly to the companies and is likely to continue after the Covid-19 Pandemic.

Credit: D MITRY

At the height of the Covid-19 Pandemic, the U.S. Department of Labor estimated that nearly a quarter of the U.S. labor force consisting of 160.7 million people was involved in the practice of working remotely. That represents around 40 million workers, up from around 5 million at the start of the Pandemic.

This 800% increase is an astonishing change that will reverberate throughout many industries. Even if more than half of those workers eventually return to commuting to company offices after the Pandemic, the resulting shift in lifestyle will have major ramifications in the Beyond the Covid Shock Economy. **The authors of this book and a number of other Economists, such as Stanford University's Nicholas Bloom, predict remote work will transform America's urban areas, eroding city centers.**

Being required to "shelter at home" by state and local governments during the Pandemic led many Americans to see the undesirable aspects in their current homes. This was especially true for those living in small urban apartments. They realized the limitations of apartment living. Although convenient to their work, especially for those workings in urban office buildings, the lack of room made "shelter at home" feel very uncomfortable and confining. Working from home productively often requires more space than is available in the average apartment. One needs a dedicated office or at least a dedicated work area. If both spouses were working at home, then two work areas were likely needed, with the areas separated to allow privacy during work. Kids that were being schooled at home also required their own area for school work. Apartment living no longer looked as attractive as it did when couples were commuting to work and kids were going to school; the search for a house, one with more space, becomes a top priority for those people that work at home.

Remote workers quickly began looking for alternative homes that could be more enjoyable if they were going to spend all day working from home. They realized they needed more space. They also realized their kids needed more space, a backyard, to replace public playgrounds and school yards that were shut down during the Pandemic. *People were on the move.* The search for more space generated a significant rise in demand for suburban and rural homes that are an easy car ride from major cities while escaping the undesirable aspects of city living.

Similarly, the demand for homes in areas of vacation destinations increased as remote workers quickly realized that working at home provided more freedom and more time to enjoy the amenities in typical vacation locations. If you liked the beach, you could take a quick trip to it, with the kids in the afternoon and catch up on your work in the evening. If you enjoyed skiing, a quick trip to the slopes in the afternoon refreshed you to be more productive. All of a sudden, these remote workers looked at favorite vacation destinations as potential homes once freed from the daily commute to the office. The consumer demand for this type of housing will also continue in the Beyond the Covid Shock Economy.

People also observed the reaction of other people during a major crisis, and they decided on things that they would want in their homes. A yard that was large enough for growing a vegetable garden that could supply the family during disruptions in supplies to local food markets became desirable. It would also be a nice place to take a short break from work, or even to do remote work from, if the weather was nice. Similarly, many people have decided they wanted more space for food storage and more space for storage of other supplies that can become less available during an upheaval in supply chains and/or panic shopping that empty store shelves for extended periods of time.

The sight of the empty store shelves, a new experience for many people, especially those in urban areas, caused people to no longer take it for granted that stores would have what they needed or in certain case would even be open for business. A larger home with more storage space, a garden for fresh vegetables and fruit, a place that is located away from urban crowds, this new perspective started to look very desirable.

The result was that large cities, such as San Francisco, Seattle, New York, Philadelphia, soon experienced a sizable exodus during the Pandemic. Many city dwellers moved to suburbs or even other states. Moving companies could not keep up with demand. As occupancy rates collapsed, rents for urban apartments quickly fell by 20% to 35% in many urban areas. Not only was the exodus the result of remote workers who saw the prospect that the benefits of remote work would become permanent after Covid. The realization was also coming to those who worked in the restaurants, cafes, shops, and other businesses that had originally emerged to support the large office buildings. Recognizing those jobs would never return to the office buildings, due to the shift to remote work, they left the city to seek better prospects elsewhere. Many will likely find jobs in the expanded suburbs as employees and newly located businesses supporting the new remote workers.

Proposals by cities government officials to replace the lost tax revenues by adding new taxes will accelerate the exodus from those urban areas. An example is New York City's proposal of a three dollar tax on all package deliveries. Here again we can see government officials making mistakes as they lack the knowledge of Economics.

Deciding to move out of a city is not a minor change; it is often a permanent one, one that will have long lasting impacts on both the cities that people leave and the new destinations to which they relocate. This is especially true when these urban dwellers replace their apartments and condos by buying single family homes in other states. The ramifications of this new migration on urban, suburban, and rural areas will be discussed in Chapter 7 on Human Geography. However, here in this Chapter, the impact of this trend on consumer lifestyles is discussed.

Instead of seeing homes as an investment or just a place to rest after working, the remote workers will see these homes as the very center of their lifestyles. They will want to create home office areas that are both productive and comfortable. High-Speed Internet will become a necessity instead of an option, along with spaces designed to function as work centers. Gardens will come back into fashion both as places for relaxation and for fresh grown food. Interior decoration will become more important as remote workers will want the most pleasant environments to work in.

Remote workers will also be looking for communities where they will be able to live a less stressful lifestyle. Morning and afternoon hikes, bike rides and running will be activities that will replace the time previously wasted on daily city commutes. This will make the proximity of parks, playgrounds, and nature trails especially attractive to those searching for "remote work homes." Small nearby neighbor restaurants and cafes for a quick relaxing break or a pleasant lunch will also be amenities desired. With a shift to more in-home entertainment along with online shopping, the presence of several movie theaters and large malls will be less important as attractions and therefore less in demand.

Those individuals who like walks on the beach, skiing, or theme parks are increasingly looking for communities where they will be able to enjoy those activities regularly without a long drive. Others who like museums, live theatre or similar urban activities will want to stay in areas closer to cities because such locations allow easy travel into an urban area where such attractions are already in abundance. Just as people are clustering online around similar interests it is likely that some remote workers will cluster in communities built around favorite activities.

Another feature that will likely be part of trending lifestyles after the Covid Shock will be an abandonment of some of the pre-virus social conventions. This was also the case following the 1889 and 1918 Pandemics. History records what became known as the "Gay

Nineties" and the "Roaring Twenties" that followed the Pandemic restrictions and hardships; a similar outpouring will likely follow for years after Covid-19 lockdowns end and economic hardships receded.

## Conclusion

Reacting to the Covid-19 Pandemic, governments enforced restrictions that often prevented people from enjoying restaurants, nightclubs, beaches, recreational areas, bars, theme parks, and most other places where people might meet. Post Pandemic, after all the restrictions are significantly reduced or eliminated entirely, people will likely "let go" and relish returning to those activities with abandon. History will record this as a "New Roaring Twenties." It will be an era remembered as a cultural period much as the original "Roaring Twenties" are remembered now.

Lifestyles will be significantly different in the United States in the Great Economic Transition to the New Normal. Remote workers will lead the change replacing their current company office focused lifestyles with home-focused ones. Recreation and relaxed suburban/rural lifestyles will replace the more stressful urban lifestyles. The changes in demographics and resulting consumer consumption will forever transform communities and industry in the "New Normal" Beyond the Covid Shock and during the Great Economic Transition.

# CHAPTER 6

## Industry -Transportation, Travel and Hospitality

Nearly every industry was transformed by the Covid-19 Pandemic; however, transportation, travel and hospitality were especially stuck hard. Photographs and videos of grounded airliners, mothballed cruise ships, closures of recreational and amusement facilities, restaurants and small businesses filled the news outlets during the Pandemic. Most of these service facilities represented the lockdowns, the quarantines, along with closed state borders became features of life under restrictions that were imposed in reaction to the Covid Pandemic. The transportation, travel, and hospitality industries will be transformed for the years ahead. However, as in other areas of normal life, the future shape of these industries will be based on existing trends that became greatly accelerated by the Pandemic.

## Air Transportation

One of the most visible aspects of the Covid-19 Pandemic was its impact on transportation. The airlines were especially hard hit by the Covid Pandemic. Because of the closing of national borders and national lockdowns, air travel sales plummeted. The number of airline passengers passing through security checkpoints to board airplanes dropped by 95% overnight. Thousands of flights were cancelled due to the reduced demand. Airline fleets were grounded around the world and hundreds of airliners no longer needed by airlines were parked in storage. Although domestic air travel recovered a bit in the late springtime of 2020, it was still down by over 70%. During the peak summer season, international air travel was down by 90% according to the International Air Travel Association (IATA).

Early in the Pandemic, the IATA projected that global annual air travel would decrease by 66% in 2020 over 2019 because of the global lockdowns starting in March 2020. The global decline would be greater except for the partial return of domestic air travel in the United States and China. In the United States, airlines established new procedures to reduce the transmission by leaving alternate rows of seats unsold, adopting new cleaning procedures and installing advanced air filtration systems. These new measures resulted in a partial return of passengers, but travelers were still reluctant to fly because of the virus. New health requirements proposed "health passports" which would include proof of Covid-19 vaccination, but such requirements if implemented would reduce further the number of passengers. Added to these conditions, there was the fear of being stranded away from home because of future Pandemic lockdowns being implemented at any time.

Many countries require that arriving passengers have proof of a negative Covid-19 test taken no earlier than 72 hours before arriving at customs. Otherwise, the passenger is required to enter a specially arranged hotel room for a period of quarantine until another PCR test shows negative. The "within 72 hours" requirement does not allow for many long connections between flights. Quarantined in a security patrolled hotel room is inconvenient and can be very costly to the disembarking passenger. **All of these events mean air travel will be slow to return to previous levels. The IATA does not expect a recovery of air travel to pre-Covid Pandemic levels until after 2023.**

**However, the IATA projection does not appear to take in the likely long-term decline in business travel from the increased use of virtual business meetings and conferences. Although business travel accounts for only 12% of airline miles, most studies show business travel generates three-quarters of airline profits. Tickets prices for non-business travel will need to rise to cover the loss of revenue from the less frequent business travelers, which in turn will reduce the number on non-business travelers since they are**

far more sensitive to price increases. Add the greater hassles from new health regulations, along with virus fears by passengers, and non-business travel will decline. It is possible that air travel, especially international air travel, may take several more years to reach the levels before the Covid-19 Pandemic.

The IATA projection does not appear to include the possible long-term impact of shortening global supply chains on air cargo demand. Globally air cargo only accounts for about 10% of airline revenues. Although air cargo will recover more quickly than passenger air service, it faces a serious long-term decline as supply chains are shortened to make them more robust. As a result of the Covid-19 lockdowns and border closing, the global demand for air cargo dropped by 17% in June 2020 from June 2019 figures. Because of the grounding of passenger flights, there was a drastic drop in cargo capacity, and the airlines actually added cargo flights. The lack of passenger flights to carry air cargo also resulted in some passenger aircraft being pressed into service to carry only mail and cargo with mail bags often strapped into passenger seats.

One immediate consequence was that the demand for commercial airliners plunged. There was no need for the large fleets of the airlines thus aircraft were immediately put in storage. Many of the older models will never fly again going directly from storage to scrapping. With the decline in passengers, the demand for new airliner sales also dropped, and contracts were cancelled. For example, Boeing cancelled its plans for building 1,050 planes during 2020 because of the lack of airline orders and even the previous backlog of unfilled orders was in serious doubt. Boeing had to lay off over 30,000 of its employees. Tens of thousands of workers that supply Boeing with aircraft components were also laid off.

The effect of these layoffs in the airline industry will ripple throughout the whole economy. For example, less demand for flights will mean less demand for aviation fuel. Aviation fuel accounted for eight percent of global oil demand, a figure expected to fall by 70% due to the Covid-19 Pandemic. Fewer air travelers will mean reduced demand for hotels, rental cars, taxis, luggage, all ancillaries associated with air travel. Although air cargo decreased by only 32% due to the Covid-19 Pandemic, it has the potential for a more sustained declined through the shortening of global supply chains. The trend towards virtual meetings and conferences along with the impact of shortened supply chains means it will be a long road back before airlines regain the traffic lost, if they ever do, and a long time before they start ordering aircraft in the numbers they had ordered before the Covid-19 Pandemic. When you add the new climate change regulations and changing public attitudes about air travel, it is possible the airline industry will never return to its former levels. A recovery of the airline industry will depend on Post Pandemic attitudes towards non-business travel, the cost and regulation of air travel, and how aggressively airlines adapt their business models to the requirements of the Post Pandemic Economy.

The decline in the airline industry will have a significant impact on the American economy. In the United States, the U.S. Federal Aviation Administration reports that 5% of the GDP is linked directly and indirectly to the air travel industry through employment at airlines, manufacture of aircraft, services provided to the airlines and services provided to air travelers and indirectly though the goods and services those workers buy in their communities. All together the air travel industry generated an estimated 11 million jobs of the estimated 132 million Americans employed in 2019. It will likely take several years for this industry to recover to previous levels.

To recover the airlines will need to start doing serious research in order to understand the needs and fears of Post Pandemic air travelers. Next, the airlines must determine the best way to address the new variables. Airlines will need to quantify the decline of business travel due to the increased use of virtual meetings and conferences along with remote work. Airlines will need to revise their business models. Since business travelers generate most of their profits, airlines will need to determine how to increase profits on vacation travel and other non-business travel.

Reluctance of air travelers to be crowded into tight seating will require airlines to rethink their models based on passenger capacity in airlines. Airlines will also need to develop strategies for promoting travel when the cost per ticket will be higher, the passengers' documents required to fly will increase, and the fact that passengers will still have a residual fear of catching a virus on a flight. The total result will be an airline industry that is leaner, smaller, highly adapted to the consumers' new requirements, and more efficient than existed prior to the Covid Pandemic, especially in terms of international air service.

## Rail and Bus Transport

The challenge in terms of the Covid-19 Pandemic for rail and bus systems is that travelers spend an extended length of time in crowded seating with individuals being much closer than six feet from other passengers. This proximity significantly increases the risk of infection by the virus. Although everyone might comply with the order to wear masks, there is no requirement that for all the masks to be of high value (N-95 or higher). The minimum separation of six feet is not likely possible even if alternate rows are used for seating. The requirement is at least six feet front, sides and back. That is a circle of over six feet in diameter. When is the last time you saw this much space in inside of a train or bus? Economically it does not pay for carriers to be retrofitted to assure that degree of separation. The only accommodation is by fewer seats sold, and staggered front to back, and all seats be numbered by tickets. This is not economically feasible for extended periods of service.

Rail passenger service in America was impacted nearly as drastically as airline service by the Pandemic. Amtrak trains, after years of growth saw ridership fall by over 80% because of lockdowns and individuals choosing to social distance. Service frequency on most routes has been cut in half and Amtrak expects ridership to be down by 37% for the 2020-2021 fiscal year. Although railroads, like airlines, installed new air filtration, social distancing by alternating seating and mask requirements to reduce the risk of transmission it will still be a while before fear of travel on railroads will bring traffic levels back to the pre-Pandemic levels. One major factor will be if the U.S. Congress provides the funding to restore Amtrak service to levels it was before the Pandemic struck.

Similarly, like the railroads, intercity bus travel declined due to the Covid-19 Pandemic and ridership on Greyhound Lines dropped by 65% at the start of the Pandemic. As with airlines and railroads bus ridership will take a while to rebound, but because intercity bus riders often have no alternatives, it will probably rebound much quicker.

## Mass Transit

Transit systems in urban areas were especially hard hit by the Pandemic lockdowns by urban areas. At the height of the first Pandemic wave, ridership on most transit systems dropped by 75% to 90%. By the time of the writing of this book, late fall 2020, ridership only returned to 40% with the prospect of it falling again as a new wave of the Pandemic generates the likelihood of future urban lockdowns. As with Intercity trains and buses, social distancing is nearly impossible on any mass transit system. Add in the large ridership in urban areas, in New York alone the subway had over 5.5 million riders per day, and crowded mass transit systems are the ideal environment for the spread of a respiratory virus like Covid-19. It is no wonder that eastern urban areas like New York, Boston, and Philadelphia were hit so hard by the virus. By June of 2020, there were 383,000 *confirmed* Covid-19 cases but sampling by the New York Department of Health in April indicated that the actual number of Covid-19 cases in the New York metropolitan area was closer to 3,000,000.

Although transit systems have initiated increased sanitation measures, better air filtration, and required shields for operators and made masks mandatory, it is likely that the effectiveness of these actions will be limited. Consider the lack of social distancing, the amount of time spent in proximity to other riders and the crowded conditions on most urban transit systems during peak hours. Therefore, the first requirement for a return to full demand for mass transit ridership is that a critical mass of immunity in the population is reached. According to experts, around 70% of the population needs to become immune, arising from either vaccination or natural immunity from surviving the virus.

However, long term it is unlikely that mass transit will return to the same levels it was at before the Pandemic. It should be recognized that prior to the Covid-19 Pandemic mass transit, especially in eastern urban areas, was declining due to competition from rideshare services like Uber and Lyft. In New York City had already declined from a high of 6 million riders in 2015 to 5.6 million by 2018. The movement to remote work, decline of urban office complexes and expansion of rideshare services due to fear of viruses will accelerate the decline of mass transit in America.

## Freight Transport

While passenger rail service sharply declined because of the Covid Pandemic, it was a different story with railroad freight. Although rail freight, in terms of carloads, declined by 8.5% in the first ten months of 2020 compared to 2019 because of Pandemic lockdowns it quickly rebounded when they ended. This was because most of the decline was due to a reduction in demand for commodities as factories closed. By contrasted the increase in demand for consumer goods resulted in an 11.5% increase in carloads of containers transported by rail. By November, when the winter wave of Covid-19 started, overall freight traffic had increased by two and a half percent over the same period in 2019. Long term railroads are likely to benefit from a shortening of supply chains. Although rail traffic from the major seaports will decline due to shortening supply chains, it will be replaced by the increase demand for domestic commodities and manufacturing.

Trucking is another transportation sector that saw only a slight decline in demand as the lockdowns occurred, followed by a rebound. During the Covid-19 Pandemic truckers emerged as heroes as they held the supply chain together delivering goods to keep supermarkets and essential stores open. Despite having to deal with a lack of restaurants, and closed rest areas, truckers kept the goods flowing from suppliers to retail outlets and homes. With the huge increase in online shopping, the trucking industry became even more critical to keeping the economy moving.

As supply chains shift onshore and remote workers leave urban areas to the extended suburbs the trucking industry will become even more important because of its flexibility to adapt to the changes in the Beyond Covid Shock Economy. One measure of the expected future success of the industry is that orders for new trucks were up 300% in November 2020 over truck sales in 2019. Trucking, always a critical industry, will be even more critical during the economic recovery as part of the Great Economic Transition.

## Global Travel Recommendations

At the start of the Covid-19 Pandemic, the following declaration was posted on the CDC's website:

> "Travel increases your chance of getting and spreading COVID-19. **Staying home is the best way to protect yourself and others from COVID-19.** You can get COVID-19 during your travels. You may feel well and not have any symptoms, but you can still spread COVID-19 to others. You and your travel companions (including children) may spread COVID-19 to other people including your family, friends, and community for 14 days after you were exposed to the virus. Don't travel if you are sick or if you have been around someone with COVID-19 in the past 14 days. Don't travel with someone who is sick."

The admonishment of **"Don't travel with someone who is sick"** is understandable, but you cannot know who may be spreading virus on any type of public transportation. Essentially and strictly speaking, this appears to leave you with your personal vehicles of transportation, echoed in different formats on the websites of other government health agencies worldwide, announcing similar quarantines and closing of borders worldwide. Although deemed necessary to stop the further spread of the virus, the result was devastating for the $2.9 trillion-dollar global travel industry.

Almost instantly, travel and tourism stopped worldwide. Wildlife parks in Africa closed to tourism, as did ski resorts in Europe. Island tourist destinations closed their borders, requiring two-week quarantines for travel. Large numbers of transatlantic flights were cancelled, and many surviving flights only carried mail and/or international travelers being allowed repatriation to their home countries under strict quarantine rules. Global travel, which had enjoyed unending growth since the end of World War II, entered a new era almost overnight, an era of quarantines, closing borders and widespread fear of travel.

## Cruise Travel Industry

The Cruise industry was one of the first devastated by the Covid-19 Pandemic. It illustrates well the impact on the global travel industry. The market for cruising suffered from the very beginning of the virus outbreak. Early in March of 2020, two ships, the "Diamond Princess" and the "Grand Princess", were quarantined, with numerous passengers infected. News outlets reported numerous ships that were refused port entries and were denied debarkation of passengers.

Television news programs broadcast video Images of passengers stuck at sea long after their tours were over, unable to return home due to closed borders. Americans on the "Diamond Princess" were eventually evacuated by the U.S. Air Force and brought to an Air Force facility in San Antonio, Texas, to wait out a two-week quarantine before being allowed to return home.

Before being evacuated to their home countries, ships passengers had been quarantined to their cabins. These wayfarers were most often confined to exceedingly small cabins for which they had paid. They were not allowed to leave and walk around the ship. Anyone who has ever taken a cruise is familiar with ship cabins and knows that unless one had reserved one of the few most expensive cabins, the space of ordinary cabins is tight quarters. These passengers would suffer claustrophobia from being confined for many weeks in their tiny spaces during quarantine.

In the USA, the CDC public health agency said that the enclosed spaces and prolonged engagement were responsible for the contagion on ships. On March 13, 2020 the Cruise Lines International Association, which encompasses all the major cruise lines, including Carnival, Royal Caribbean, MSC and Norwegian, announced the cruise line members would suspend United States operations for 30 days. The suspension of tour operations was then extended again and again, month after month. At first, the cruise lines were looking toward early 2021 for reopening, but then that changed to 2022. Many in the industry wonder if the decline in popularity of cruise vacations will ever fully recover. Like the damage to health caused by the virus, the financial impact was injurious Carnival Corporation stock sank to $11 per share, down from $51 price. Royal Caribbean Cruises Ltd. dropped to $28 down from $135. Norwegian Cruise Line Holdings dropped to $10, down from the $59 peak in January. The companies had to borrow large sums of money on their lines of credit.

In July of 2020, Carnival Corporation announced that the company would be selling 13 ships across its portfolio of cruise lines. Holland America Line indicated it would be selling four cruise ships. Carnival Cruise Line confirmed media reports that ships named "Carnival Fantasy" and "Carnival Inspiration" would be scrapped in Turkey. Former Royal Caribbean ships "Sovereign of the Seas" and "Monarch of the Seas" were also beached in a breaker yard at Aliaga, Turkey, to be scrapped.

The Covid-Era marked a time for revision of cruise line planning and the industry's future. The corporate executives had assembled specialists to develop optimal plans for safe operations when cruise lines were ordered to stop operations because of Covid-19 lockdowns. Cruise companies then initiated procedures aimed at mitigating viral spread onboard vessels. Creative planning was a major effort for cruise line management. Some plans required considerable re-imagining of operations. Here again we see that in a competitive market economy innovation arises and provides opportunities for a turnaround based on intensive planning.

Credit: Pexel – Diego F. Parra

Viking Ocean Cruises completed the installation of the first full-scale Covid-19 testing laboratory on a cruise ship. This onboard facility testing capacity enables Viking to conduct testing of all crew members and all guests with a non-invasive Covid-19 saliva test. The laboratory has the capacity to test every crew member and guest daily. The capacity for testing provides the flexibility to respond to Covid-19 prevalence levels wherever the ship travels worldwide. However, testing is only a stop gap measure and will likely have limited impact on public attitudes towards cruise ship as havens for disease.

The Post Pandemic Economy will no doubt be a time of reduced availability of cruises since demand for such travel will diminish from fear of the virus. The trend towards larger cruise ships will probably be reversed and cruises will more often be local instead of transoceanic. What will the market in the Post Pandemic era look like for cruise lines? Ship practices, procedures, agreements with ports, and innovations in handling potential for spread of infections will become the new standard in business aboard ships. Look for the popularity of cruise vacations to slowly return and move toward the previous level. The Cruise Industry, like other industries, will not die but will adapt to the Post Pandemic Economy. Nevertheless, it will be a slow recovery to reach a "New Normal" for these companies.

The Cruise industry is just one very visible example of the huge impact of the Pandemic on the travel industry. Tourist destinations like Hawaii, Jamaica, the Greek Islands, South Pacific, Hong Kong, Macau, and Las Vegas saw the number of tourists drop to almost nothing overnight. Casinos and Resorts were closed under lockdown orders. Conventions and Conferences, a major source of revenue source for many cities were canceled outright or moved online. Beaches were closed, Theme Parks were closed, Zoos and Aquariums were closed. Hotel occupancy rates dropped to under 20% in many cities. Although some visitors returned during the summer of 2020 as the first wave of the virus waned, the lockdowns and capacity restrictions in late autumn and winter generated a new round of impacts on the travel industry. At the point of this writing, it is expected that these travel restrictions will last well into 2021, generating a loss year for the travel industry.

**The magnitude of the impact on the travel industry means that the fallout will actually last for decades, and is a major force shaping the Beyond the Covid shock Economy.** Recovery will come slow due to a combination of new travel regulations and a latent fear among tourists following the Pandemic. Domestic travel destinations, especially those in within the range of domestic autos, will recover first followed by international destinations.

The speed of recovery will depend on the structure of the new health regulations for travel in the Post Pandemic Economy. It will also depend on how comfortable tourists feel and weather they believe that the Covid-19 virus has been placed under control or possibly eliminated. It will also depend on how much disposable income tourists have as the economy recovers. The less disposable income individuals have, the less likely they are to travel far from home. The Pandemic lockdowns and consequent increase in unemployed result in a serious decline in consumers' disposable income.

## Hospitality

The hospitality industry was also devastated by the Covid-19 Pandemic. During the first wave, hotel and motels were virtually empty due to the lack of travelers. Some local governments took advantage of the empty units to house the homeless in order to protect homeless street people from the virus. After the first wave of the Pandemic waned, travelers returned to using hotels, but the number was a fraction of the numbers prior to the Pandemic. Hotels and resorts that depended on conventions and conference remained mostly empty as these meetings continued to be canceled or moved online. New sanitation requirements were put in place, but these also increased the cost of housekeeping.

The future of many hotels and motels depends on how soon the Covid-19 virus is brought under control and travelers return. Based on the resurgence of the virus as this book is written demand will probably not start to return until late springtime 2021, representing a more than a lost year for the industry. Many properties will probably not survive. Those that do will have higher costs from the new sanitation practices and lower revenues from lower occupancy rates, fewer patrons because of fear of traveling and/or lacking income to travel. The business models will have to adapt to these realities if these businesses wish to survive. One option optimal for desirable tourist destinations might be to reposition them to attract remote workers seeking prolonged stays. Extended stay might be an optimal choice attractive to workers seeking more desirable or even exotic locations.

## Restaurant Industry

Restaurants were another group of businesses that were struck hard by the Covid-19 lockdowns and capacity restrictions. The restaurant industry suffered "in extremis". During the strictest lockdowns, traditional dining was banned, and the only option restaurants had to stay in business was curbside service, restaurant pickups, or home delivery. Although, the restrictions on restaurants were somewhat relaxed after the first wave of the Covid-19 Pandemic waned, there was another problem. The new sanitation and air filtration requirements increased costs while the capacity limits, often at 50% or less than pre-Covid-19 Pandemic level, severely reduced revenues. The resulting squeeze meant that most restaurants continued to lose money.

Again, shutdowns were ordered during the autumn and winter and this eliminated even the modest on-site dining options for many restaurants nationwide. As a result, it is estimated more than half of restaurants nationwide will go out of business in the United States.

Many famous restaurant chains have already gone bankrupt. Others will follow before the Pandemic is completely over. Those restaurants that do survive, lessons learned, will be operating with drastically different business models in the Post Pandemic World.

During the Pandemic lockdowns, many customers started purchasing restaurant takeout meals, which increased takeout by 60-70% from before the Pandemic. Overnight this option used by only a small segment of the market became common practice. Other people turned to home delivery and consequently new home delivery services boomed. As with most innovations, once a habit is established among consumers, it tends to persist and become routine. As a result, most restaurants should now expect that some combination of meals for pickup and home delivery will need to be a standard part of their business fare.

Although diners will definitely return once restaurants are reopened, it is likely the numbers of customers will be fewer because of changes in work patterns and lifestyles following the Pandemic. The first consideration will be the decline in the number of travelers. Restaurants that depend on tourism will need to compete hard for the reduced number of tourists.

The second change is the increased trend towards remote work. Restaurants that depended on urban office workers for revenue will find there will be a lot fewer of these workers after the Pandemic. These urban restaurants will need to adapt their business model for the changed composition of urban areas in the United States.

The third outcome is that remote workers are more likely to eat at home or nearby, increasing demand in the expanded suburban areas for restaurants that do curbside pickup and home delivery.

The last trend from the latent fears remaining after the Pandemic also means that patrons in restaurants will likely prefer outdoor dining or large booths that separate diners. Many will avoid buffets. Many restaurants will go under before the culture settles into the "New Normal", but the ones that survive and adapt will be well positioned to be successful after the Pandemic is over.

## Light at the end of the Tunnel

Beyond the return of tourists, the movement towards remote work will also shape the future of the travel industry. Instead of quick vacation trips of a week or two to favorite destinations by travelers that must soon return to fixed worksites, remote workers will be free to remain at a given spot for prolonged periods, working wherever they have Internet access.

This new breed "the remote work tourist" was evident in the summer of 2020 when many remote workers, fleeing New York City, spent weeks and even months living in traditional vacation towns on Long Island. Many workers stayed remained "in situ" well into the autumn season beyond the normal tourist season in order to avoid future Pandemic restrictions. K-12 students attending classes online also enabled these families to extend their "vacations" for months.

Credit: Pexel – Katsuma

**Conclusion** **As the percentage of remote workers increase, these prolonged stays at tourist destinations will increase. Remote workers who enjoy skiing will relocate to their favor ski regions during ski season. Other remote workers who dread winter months will join the traditional retiree snowbirds, and travel south for the winter. At the same time, remote workers living in southern communities and southwestern deserts will "migrate" to the mountains and some northern communities in the summer season.**

A new industry of "resident tourism" will develop to serve this new demographic. Some of the more adventurists might even "migrate" to foreign destinations like the Caribbean or Canada during the appropriate season although these remote workers might run afoul of international tax regulations written before the emergence of remote work.

# CHAPTER 7

## Industry - Retailing, Energy, Internet Services, and Robotics

Retailing, Energy, Internet Services, and Robotic Technology are additional industries that will be transformed by the experiences of the Covid-19 Pandemic. The trends shaping the future of these industries are not new; they already existed well before the Pandemic struck. However, these trends were all accelerated by the related Pandemic lockdowns and the spread of the virus. The accelerated trends will have a major role in shaping the Post Pandemic Economy.

### Retailing

Retailing was another industry transformed by the Pandemic lockdowns. The closing of retailers deemed non-essential and restrictions of the number of customers allowed inside stores during lockdowns drove many customers to shop online or use curbside pickup. In addition to more customers shopping online, especially older Americans in the high-risk category for the virus, the purchase volume of the average household increased. In addition, the type of online purchases shifted in favor of clothing, groceries, and office supplies, accelerating the trend of consumers shopping online.

In the Fourth Quarter of 2019, prior to the global emergence of the Covid-19 virus, online shopping accounted for around 11.4% of all retail sales in the United States according to the U.S. Census Bureau. The $158 billion in ecommerce sales was a 16.7% increase over ecommerce sales in the Fourth Quarter of 2018, reflecting a quarter century trend in online shopping. By the height of the Covid virus lockdowns in the $2^{nd}$ Quarter of 2020, ecommerce sales increased to over $200 Billion, an increase of 44.4% from the Second Quarter of 2019. Ecommerce sales accounted for 15.1% of total retail sales.

In the Third Quarter of 2020, after the first wave of lockdowns ended for the most part, ecommerce sales decreased only slightly to $199.4 Billion from the Second Quarter, a figure that still represented a 37.1% increase from the Third Quarter of 2020. This trend indicated that although consumers did return to the stores when they opened, many still retained the newer habit of buying online that was acquired during the Pandemic. **The trend to online shopping was greatly accelerated by the Covid-19 Pandemic and**

**gains in ecommerce are likely to be permanent as consumers retain their new shopping habits.**

Sales increased not only at online retailers like Amazon, but also for traditional retailers like Walmart that used curbside pickup. In the Second Quarter Walmart saw its online sales increase by 74%, mostly for groceries items bought curbside. Many supermarkets also expanded curbside service. Although the trend in curbside service in retailing was expanding for years, the lockdown accelerated it significantly. Numerous grocery shoppers that used "pickup" throughout the lockdowns found using it to be extremely easy and convenient. Consumers could select their groceries at leisure online from home without the distractions of point-of-purchase displays or having to walk long distances searching in the store or waiting in long checkout lines. Instead, customers are able to select quickly the items they need, directly from their shopping list online. When the customers arrive curbside, the purchases are loaded for them into the trunks of their cars. The customers do not even need get out of their vehicles. It is a brisk and convenient way to shop. Having become accustomed to it throughout Pandemic lockdowns, many consumers will continue to use curbside pickup as a choice.

**The Covid-19 Pandemic has transformed the retailing industry permanently. Millions of customers now shop online, the purchases delivered directly or as curbside pickup. This serves most of their retail**

**needs.** The Pandemic lockdowns accelerated the trend towards online shopping, not only for traditional retail goods but also for grocery shopping at supermarkets. As a result, even the smallest retailers in order to survive will have to adopt online retailing and online order options. **Because of the Pandemic, online shopping went from being a specialize part of retailing to part of the retailing mainstream (expect this trend to increase quickly to over 20% of retail sales and continue upward). Similarly, the trend of curbside shopping will be an important element of the retail strategy of supermarkets in the Post Pandemic Economy.** Likely curbside will account for more than 25% of sales for these businesses.

## Energy Industry and the Oil Market

It was a day no one in the oil industry thought would ever come, negative oil prices. On Monday, April 20, 2020, the prices for futures contracts on crude oil scheduled for May delivery dropped to negative $37.63 a barrel from a price of around $60 barrel at the start of the year. With trading scheduled to end on Tuesday April 21, 2020, falling demand from Pandemic lockdowns and a price war between Saudi Arabia and Russia had wiped out the market for May oil futures. June oil futures were still trading at a price of $20.43. Still, the psychological damage had been done.

Global demand for oil had been rising steadily until the Covid-19 virus stuck. The first signs of trouble for oil was in January when demand for oil in China collapsed due to the lockdown of the Chinese economy. Soon storage tanks in China became full, and oil tankers started to back up in Chinese ports from a lack of space to offload their oil. Then this "oil glut" spread around the world with the Covid-19 virus.

In 2019, the global demand for oil averaged around 100 million barrels a day. At the height of the first wave of the Pandemic in April 2020, it fell by 29 million barrels to only 71 million barrels per day, a level not seen since 1995.

The grounding of airlines, docked cruise ships, urban lockdowns eliminating commuter rush hours and "shelter at home" orders that eliminated store shopping trips had all combined to cut demand for oil worldwide. Although G20 Energy Ministers and the Ministers of the Organization for Petroleum Exporting Countries (OPEC) worked together on a strategy for stabilizing world oil markets, it took a while for production to scale back to meet the new much lower demand. Although oil demand is expected to rebound as Covid-19 vaccines allow the economy to recover, the demand for oil will take a while to reach the same levels it was prior to the Covid-19 Pandemic for due to structural changes in the Beyond the Covid Shock Economy. **Indeed, the British energy firm, BP, has declared that it is very possible 2019 will be the historical year of peak oil for some time. There are strong arguments for peak oil demand having already been reached, or be-**

ing close, given the likely structure of the Post Pandemic Economy.

Remote work will reduce the demand for gasoline as it eliminates the daily commute for millions of workers. Regardless if the commute is by automobile, mass transit or a combination of the two, such diminished travel means less demand for oil.

Similarly, a reduction in demand for air travel arising from a combination of virtual meetings, reduced tourism and health regulations will reduce the demand for jet fuel. The shortening of global manufacturing supply chains to make them more robust will reduce demand for global cargo transports by both air and ships, again reducing the demand for oil.

The adoption of high yield Controlled Agriculture Environment technology to shorten agricultural supply chains will shorten the distance food travels to reach consumers. The need for petroleum-based pesticides will also be reduced as farmers move to the frontier of high-tech agriculture, further reducing the demand for oil.

**Together these trends of the Post Pandemic Economy will reduce global demand for oil. The purchase of electric automobiles, electric trucks, and the use of biofuels in aviation will reduce demand even further. If producers become reluctant to restore production to Pre-Covid levels after being hit by the Covid-Era price shock the oil supply will also remain low, so lower demand may not translate into lower oil prices**

in the new Post Pandemic Economy, delaying the return to Pre-Covid demand levels. All of these are strong arguments that peak oil production was reached in 2019. At the very least, it will take oil a while to recover to the 2019 production levels.

Furthermore, that assumes no new detrimental government regulations on U.S. oil production. Otherwise, a reversal of the trend leading the U.S. to oil independence will have severe economic consequences.

## COAL

The global demand for coal also declined because of the Covid Pandemic and the associated lockdowns. With factories, shopping malls and office buildings closed, the demand for electricity declined steeply. Since a quarter of electricity in the United States is generated by using coal, the demand for it dropped. Internationally 41% of electricity is generated by coal. The International Energy Agency projected a 5% drop in demand for electricity and an 8% drop in global demand for coal in 2020 with recovery in 2021. However, such predictions of coal recovery are based on a return to a pre-Pandemic economy (the "Old Normal").

However, the acceleration of online shopping, remote work, and migration from urban to rural areas as features of the Post Pandemic Economy will undoubtedly result in a slower recovery of demand for electricity. The expansion of renewable energy will likely provide for most of the increased demand for electricity. The result will be a continuation of the gradual decline of domestic demand for coal. **This means the Post Pandemic recovery of the coal industry will be slow driven by a decreasing domestic demand for coal, although foreign nations will drive demand upward as their economies recover.**

## Natural Gas

Natural gas was impacted by the first wave of the Covid-19 virus. Accounting for 38% of the electricity generation in the United States, the demand was hit by the lockdowns during the first wave of the virus. The price for natural gas declined throughout the first wave of the Pandemic to a record low of $1.66 MMBtu (Million Metric British thermal units) in February 2020 but recovered at $2.89 MMBtu by November 2020.

Natural gas is seen as a transition fuel to a renewable economy and so the long-term impact of the Pandemic on it will be less than for coal or oil. The continual conversion of coal power plants to natural gas and the building of new power plants will support market demand even as patterns of energy use change in the Post Pandemic Economy. The construction of pipelines and Liquid Natural Gas (LNG) terminals at seaports will create export opportunities for natural gas, generating additional long-term demand.

# Renewable energy

The expansion of renewable energy use in the United States will continue in the Post Pandemic Economy. Driven by a desire to reduce CO2 emissions, the employment of wind tribunes, solar power and perhaps new alternatives may be the energy of choice as the economy adapts and expands.

Unlike fossil fuels, wind and solar energy, once installed, requires less labor to operate. Unlike coal and oil, once installed, neither solar nor wind power are dependent on long labor intense supply chains. These features are desirable attributes in a world that will fear outbreaks of future pandemics. They are also more suitable to decentralization which fits into the other decentralization trends like remote work and modern automated factories.

Currently, the alternative sources to fossil fuels still remain more expensive sources of energy, and they also depend on locations suitable for operation that are limited, but it is possible that increased research will work to make one or the other more efficient and less expensive. Only when this economic requirement is reached, can a much larger percentage of reliable energy come from solar and wind.

## Internet Products & Services

One sector of the economy that prospered from the Covid-19 Pandemic was wireless communications and the companies involved in providing Internet services. Internet providers, computer manufacturers, video conferencing providers, computer accessory providers and streaming services have all benefited from the Pandemic lockdowns.

The overnight shift to remote work and online learning created a huge demand for the products and services of this sector. In the case of hardware providers, supply chains nearly collapsed as retailers ran out of the computers and webcams needed for remote work. A trip to the stores that were still allowed to be open showed how much the supply-chains were damaged. For example, the "big-box stores" selling computers and accessories had rows of empty shelves (nothing to show) for months. The service suppliers had their networks overwhelmed by demand.

Prior to 2020, few individuals outside the tech world had heard of a company called "Zoom." In December of 2019, there were 19 million individuals per day using its video conferencing system. Quickly, the number of viewers exploded to over 300 million per day by April 2020, a 1600% increase. Because it is easy to remember its name and the ease of use, Zoom became the symbol of virtual meetings during the Pandemic. The stock price of Zoom reflected its success, going from $68.72 a share on January 2, 2020 to a high of $568.34

on October 19, 2020 before retreating for a while into the $400 range. This stock was just one among several video conferencing investments that benefited from the Pandemic, and "Zoom" is one of the companies now positioned to take advantage of the opportunities in the Post Pandemic Economy.

Internet providers of course benefited as the use of the Internet surged in the lockdowns. A global survey by Kaspersky Consultants showed that Internet use of social media by Millennials increased two hours a day during lockdowns, from five hours to seven hours. Both remote work and the increased use of streaming services like Netflix, Hulu and Amazon Prime created additional demand for high-speed Internet providers. Rural areas were especially hard hit by the lack of high-speed Internet.

Not only did the rural shortage of high-speed Internet create barriers to remote work and video conferencing in rural America it also made online learning by students nearly impossible. In many areas rural school districts had to resort to turning school buses into Internet hotspots in order to provide limited services to students. In inner city areas, the high cost of Internet services also created barriers to online learning and remote work. Public/private partnerships will need to be created to ensure that affordable high-speed Internet is available to every home in the United States. High-speed Internet will be as essential as electricity in the Post Pandemic Economy.

The overnight shift to remote work and online learning created an immediate shortage in home computer systems, webcams, and other necessities of a home office. The shortage was made worst due to the shutdown of factories and closing of borders in China during the first weeks of the Covid-19 Pandemic. The clustering of most of the electronic manufacturing in China created a worldwide shortage just when computer hardware was needed the most by global markets. It continues to make the world's electronic supplies vulnerable to future lockdowns in China, which is why businesses need to develop alternative sources of supply.

The collapse of computer industry supply chains resulted in a 13% decline in laptop sales during the first wave of the Pandemic and it was not until the Third Quarter of 2020 that the sales of new laptops exceeded those of the same quarter in 2019. Other shortages also emerged due to surging demand and lack of supply. The demand for webcams increased by 179% in March as remote work and online learning took hold. Retail stocks soon sold out due to the lack of supply, and webcams were being sold by third parties at prices several times retail prices. Even in the Third Quarter, the most popular webcams were difficult to find in retail outlets as manufacturers struggled to keep up with demand. **The failure of supply chains in computer hardware will be remembered for a long time, and lead to the development of more robust supply chains in the Post Pandemic Economy.**

The shift to a Post Pandemic Economy based on remote work, virtual conferencing, online learning and virtual entertainment will lead to the emergence of new industries as a result of advances in both digital technology and the digital economy. Hardware manufacturers will compete to develop better technology to increase worker productivity. Better streaming platforms will be developed virtual entertainment and virtual reality technology will be advanced to create more of an "in-person" experience. There will also be a focus on eliminating the digital divide by bringing high-speed Internet to both rural America and the inner city. Satellite constellations like SpaceX's Starlink will be part of the solution and well placed to succeed in the Post Pandemic Economy.

New companies will emerge to compete with existing online learning firms to develop improved learning platforms for the K-12 environment. Video conferencing firms will compete to develop better and more secure video conferencing technology. New consulting firms will emerge, and existing consultants will adapt their practices to assist companies in adjusting to remote work and increasing worker productivity. Other consultants will focus on organizing and supporting virtual conventions and conferences. **The Post Pandemic Economy will result in numerous opportunities for entrepreneurs to accelerate the economy's adaption to the "New Normal" of the Beyond the Covid Shock Economy. The word to pay attention to is "opportunities" considering that the Covid-19 Pandemic opened**

**the door to new business ventures to take the place of the old ventures that failed to survive the Covid-19 Pandemic.**

In the process of reacting to various problems and limitations, the producers as well as consumers of products and services were forced to direct serious attention to alternatives. These alternatives are the "ways and means" of satisfying the necessary transformation in each sector of the world's economic system. The process has been frenetic because of the alterations in the public's perceived needs. This phenomenon is a primary reason for the rapid changes in the "ways and means" that cause earlier tendencies, "trends", to intensify and to evolve as the "New Normal" after the Pandemic has passed into history.

## Technology and Product Supply chains

As readers have seen in the previous chapters of this book, the Robotics Industry will be another winner in the Post Pandemic Economy. The Pandemic illustrated the need to advance robotic technology, particularly in two areas; shortening supply chains and reducing consumer contacts. Both will have long-term impacts on the role of robots in the economy and will shape the future of the Robotics Industry.

The manufacturing of a diversity of products moved overseas the last several decades, labor costs being less than in the United States. The low cost of shipping products to the United States from aboard figures in, as well, to the picture. However, as the Pandemic showed, the complexities of global supply chains are easily disrupted by localize shutdowns of factories and the closing of international borders. The cost of lost revenues from depleted stock offset years of profits from reduced labor costs manufacturing once enjoyed. These disruptions also harmed relations between the members of the supply chains as the orders for product were delayed or not fulfilled. Both impacts are reasons for companies to rethink their global supply chain strategies by exploring options for "on-shoring" to bring manufacturing closer to its markets.

Fragile global supply chains especially impacted medical industries when their products were needed the most. Shortages of Personal Protection Equipment (PPE), pharmaceuticals and ventilators occurred not only to surging demand but also due to nations closing their borders and even seizing shipments for their own use. This illustrated that in the case of medical goods and robust supply chains that are not subject to borders being closed, while not only important to the industry but are critical to national security. In the Post Pandemic Economy, government policies must recognize this reality and encourage the production of a majority of medical products and pharmaceuticals domestically or at least within North America under the new United States – Mexico – Canada Trade Agreement (USMCA).

The Pandemic also struck the global supply chains for electronics, especially in the computer industry. When demand for computers and computer accessories surged due to the pandemic-driven shift to remote work and online learning, the products were unavailable due to shortages in the supply chain. At first, the shortages were the result of the Covid-19 virus hitting China, shutting down the factories that produced most of the world's electronics.

Then, after the lockdowns in China ended, there was a lag in crucial products being delivered because of border restrictions and the long distances of the supply chains. Companies in the computer industry, having suffered from lost revenue due to the failure of their supply chains, are apt to move production back to North America. In order to be price competitive the new factories will need to be significantly automated and to depend heavily on robotic systems driven by Artificial Intelligence (AI).

## Supply Chain impact and Technological responses

The trend instinct to replace global supply chains with shorter more regional ones is not new. Even before the Covid-19 Pandemic, firms were exploring how to shorten supply chains. As with the other trends, this tendency existed before the Covid-19, but it has been significantly accelerated. Even before Covid-19 struck, firms were under pressure to reduce the length of their supply chains due to climate change and trade wars. Government efforts to fight climate change were already focusing on global supply chains since the further a product travels to market the greater amount of greenhouse gases are released on behalf of that product.

Increasingly proposals to fight climate change involved taxes and regulations on transportation that would increase the shipping costs of good to where they would be greater than the savings from lower cost labor. Similarly, the addition of tariffs on many goods because of trade wars served to offset the lower costs of labor from global outsourcing. The disruption of the global supply chains has simply added another reason for reviewing their value and competitiveness of a brand. In order to reduce the cost of labor and remain competitive means these new factories are going to need to employ the most advanced automation and robotic systems available increasing not only the demand for automation but adding pressure to advance robotic technology and AI solutions.

Besides lowering the cost of labor in supply chains, there is another reason for companies to look at automating their production systems: the risks of future pandemics closing factories. The working conditions of many existing factories are well suited to spreading respiratory viruses like Covid-19. Numerous factories in urban areas along with slaughterhouses in rural regions were hit by the virus and were required to close. This illustrates the need to make production facilities, especially in essential industries like agriculture and medical supplies, more resistant to virus shutdowns. Following the 1918 Flu Pandemic factories were redesigned to be healthier work environments and to move outside of urban centers. The Covid-19 Pandemic will result in a similar re-evaluation of the work environment and location factories. Both automation and robotics will be the answer, and companies will be retrofitting many existing facilities to reduce the number of workers needed. New production facilities will be designed around "state of the art" automation to minimize the need for workers.

Agriculture will also be moving toward greater automation. The difficulty and additional cost of labor during the Covid-19 Pandemic will find farm operations looking at the benefits of automation. Although the focus will be on robotic harvesting technology for fruit and vegetables, another facet of agriculture will also see robotic technology as a potential way to reduce labor requirements. Farms are well suited for robotic driven tractors and drones to prepare fields, plant seeds, fertilizer, and pesticides. The expansion of Controlled Environment Agriculture will also be heavily dependent on robotic systems.

The second Covid-19 Pandemic trend that will drive technology in the robotic industry will be the desire to reduce contact with customers. The impact of Covid-19 lockdowns will inspire rideshare services, like Uber and Lyft, and taxi services to invest in robotic vehicles.

These will allow riders to reach their destinations without coming into contact with other individuals, distancing desirable in a pandemic. Commuters were already shifting from the use of mass transit systems to rideshare services before the Covid-19 Pandemic. The availability of driverless vehicles will be even more attractive as an option to mass transit.

Fast food outlets have been experimenting with various types of robotic and automatic systems to reduce costs. Recently, a new firm, Bobacino, has demonstrated a robot capable of making Boba drinks, a new drink from Asia that combines tea, milk, sweetener and little balls of "Boba" for flavoring. Other robots have demonstrated how to make coffee drinks and flip hamburgers. Systems that allow individuals to place orders and pay without human contact, have also been tested and will eventually become important to the Beyond the Covid Shock Economy.

Retailers have also been exploring the employment of robots to reduce labor costs. From stocking shelves to automated checkout stands, experiments have shown how it might be possible to reduce labor requirements in retail environments. Already large online retailers have made use of robotic systems in their warehouse. Some have even experimented with robotic drones for home delivery. The so-called "Big Box" stores have engaged robots that tread along the many isles of shelves doing inventory checks and keeping records on merchandise, instead of using human employees for this type of daily inventorying. The Pandemic has created a motivation for these experiments to be expanded. **As previously described, the process of reacting to various problems and limitations, means producers as well as consumers of products and services are *forced* to focus attention on alternatives in the various "ways and means" impacting each sector of the global economic system. These actions are a primary reason for the rapid changes of earlier tendencies to blossom into "trends" which are intensified and after the Covid-19 Pandemic has passed into history become normal.**

# Chapter 8

## Effect on Human Geography

One lasting impact of pandemics of the past was on Human Geography. The Black Death forced a migration of peoples from manor estates to inhabit villages when the labor shortage hastened the decline of the Serf System. The 1918 Flu Pandemic accelerated the expansion of suburban areas as former city dwellers left the cities, and were replaced by African Americans coming from the South and migrated to northern urban areas for work. Similarly, the 2020 Covid-19 Pandemic will have a lasting impact on Human Geography and the urban exodus of various populations.

## Impact of the Decline of Office Buildings

The rise of remote work will be one of the major drivers of the shifts in Human Geography. As more individuals work remotely, the need for enormous and expensive high-rise office buildings in urban areas will decline. This decline in the physical office workforce will create a ripple effect in the economics of urban areas. As noted in Chapter Three the trend towards remote work predates the virus but government lockdowns that forced former physical office workers to "shelter-at-home" during the early phases of the Pandemic greatly accelerated the trend. Business management could not refuse the "shelter-at-home" order and had to tell their workers to "work from home." With the original two week "shelter-at-home" extending to several months as the Covid-19 Pandemic raged, remote work became the "New Normal" for over a third of the national workforce.

First, let us take a look at the origin of the modern office building. It originated in the 19$^{th}$ Century when the expansion of railroads, banking, insurance, and stock exchanges created the need for large number of clerical workers. Because of limited communication technology of the day, only local phone service and mail, these workers were gathered into increasingly large "office factories" clustered together in major urban areas. As corporations grew and the number of "white-collar" workers started to outnumber "blue-collar" workers, the "office building" turned into a skyscraper and became a visible strength of the business that owned it. Not until the emergence of the Internet and improved digital communications was there any practical alternative to the office building.

Since the late 1990s, when the technology became available, a trend of working from home began as a cost saving measure initially by small high-tech startup companies.

In 2020, when the government authorities initiated the Covid *lockdown*, business leaders and employees thought the "shelter-at-home" mandate would be only for a brief time and then it would be back to the offices for everyone.

Originally, the "shelter-at home" was to be for a couple of weeks, but it was extended repeatedly as the infection rate remained high. During that time, many managers found that productivity and worker satisfaction increased when employees were working from home. As a result, companies quickly realized the potential of having their office workers continue working at home for an extended period, using the Internet for communications. Thousands of offices in high-rise buildings now remained vacant as the workers were working "at home." It is understandable that after digital voice, text and video communications became commonplace, most office workers actually did not need to be collected into large multistory high-rise buildings in order to accomplish ordinary daily tasks:

1. There was no need to leave one's office to communicate with someone in another office.
2. There was no need to carry a paper document from one office to another office on another floor of the huge building.

3. Fulltime trained and experienced office employees did not need the physical presence of supervisors to look over their shoulders.

Therefore, as a result advances in technology, most office workers did not need to be in confined to cubicles in office buildings. Personal computers and Internet, widely available for years, had eliminated the office paradigm since many workers could now accomplish their work from their homes. However, inertia prevented businesses from taking full advantage of the flexibility and efficiency the technology offered. The Covid-19 lockdown changed the entire complexion of global commerce by forcing business to use cyberspace to its fullest extent for remote work accelerating the adoption of it literally overnight.

Management found that all the efforts and expenses associated with keeping employees productive and happy were no longer necessary because many of them were happier and quite productive working in their homes. Everyone learned that office meetings and large gatherings in cities was not the only route for talented people to collaborate and to innovate. Workers could do so on Zoom or utilizing of the similar software programs.

Entrepreneurs and managers found new ways to use existing technologies such as Zoom, Slack, MS Teams or WebEx, and we can expect that even more sophisticated platforms will be invented. Some new software platforms may use aspects of virtual reality for meetings, which offer alternative dynamic impressions that previously existed only in live physical encounters.

## The Suburban Migration

Suburban areas will be the immediate beneficiaries of the expansion of remote work. In the case of New York, the majority of the 300,000 households moving during the first few months of the Pandemic have relocated to suburban areas within 30-40 miles of the city. Just as in the 1918 Flu Pandemic which accelerated the first migration out of cities to the suburbs, the 2020 Covid Pandemic has sparked a new migration.

Prior to the Covid Pandemic, as with the 1918 Flu Pandemic, the crowding in big cities was an attraction for a segment of the population, but the experiences of survival during the Covid-19 Pandemic and its associated lockdowns changed the view of many people as to the advantages of city life. Big city dwellers realized the crowding that they once enjoyed was now endangering their lives. With remote work eliminating a major reason to live in cities, that is to say, proximity to their offices, workers began questioning the value of an urban lifestyle. The time wasted in heavy street traffic, on crowded mass transit systems and walking on busy sidewalks became to be seen as a real burden. Add the pollution, and noise and rush of a typical city, along with higher crime rates, and life in small high-priced apartments made many individuals question if living within the city was worth it. Surely, there was a better choice for their lives.

With work life shifting to homes, remote workers wanted larger homes with gardens and dedicated space for a home office or two in the case of dual working couples. With schools, parks and recreation areas on lockdown they wanted some place their kids could play. However, they still needed to be close enough to cities for occasional physical meetings. They also wanted to be close enough to enjoy the amenities that large cities offered, making suburbs and semi-rural communities within 30 to 40 miles of urban areas especially attractive. Those workers that were able to make the move to the suburbs during the Covid-19 Pandemic are the pioneers of this new trend. They will be followed by more as it becomes clear that many employers intend to make remote work or hybrid work the norm after the Pandemic in order to save money and improve their economic efficiency to survive the Recession that the repeated waves of restrictions and lockdowns generated.

With many individuals and families moving to suburbs, builders will respond with new designs to accommodate their needs. A suburban housing boom will be generated. New homes will be designed by builders to meet the news of remote workers with semi-isolated dual home offices to enable more efficient and comfortable working areas. These will likely include direct access to garden areas for relaxing breaks, with remote workers able to spend more time at home with their families. Builders will design houses more spacious and inviting.

Businesses will follow the remote workers as they move from urban areas to the suburbs. Starbucks, which got its start as an urban coffee house, has already announced it is closing 400 urban Starbuck Cafes and replacing them with new ones in suburban areas. Likely many of tens thousands of restaurant owners who went bankrupt during the Covid-19Pandemic will decide to reopen in the newly expanding suburbs where there will be room for outdoor dining and drive-through windows. Other urban business entrepreneurs that went bankrupt during the Pandemic will likely also look at starting again in the suburbs.

Businesses that choose to employ hybrid work models will also have incentives to move to the expanding suburbs. Land will be cheaper and their offices will be more accessible to their work force making the hybrid model more viable. This will allow them to attract a higher quality work force as workers following the Pandemic focus more on lifestyle and family.

Large central office buildings could be replaced with numerous satellite facilities in suburban areas linked together by advanced communication technology.

As manufacturing firms look to shorten supply chains by on-shoring production, they will also look to the newly expanding suburbs. Their proximity to major ports in the nearby urban areas and lower density populations, not to mention risk from shutdowns in future pandemics, will make suburbs attractive for the new high-tech manufacturing facilities and future supply chains hubs.

## Reinventing Cities

With the exodus of office workers abandoning urban areas to working remotely, the overall nature of cities will change in the Post Pandemic Economy. Although some pundits will proclaim the decline of the office skyscraper and acceleration of remote work, the fact is the death of the city will not exactly be the case. Throughout history, cities have followed a cycle of being reinvented as the economy changed. This will be true of the Post Pandemic Economy as well.

In the past, innovations were closely associated with urbanization. There were good reasons for that association. For example, larger cities could enable larger gatherings. The common accessibility of human physical interaction provided the sharing of information and ideas, and this was responsible for much innovation. Originally, trading centers for agricultural products, cities evolved into trading centers for manufactured products as agricultural markets were driven to the outlying fringes by high land costs. Then in the 19$^{th}$ Century, high land costs drove the trading and manufacturing of goods to the

**outlying fringes and they were replaced by the expansion of banking and clerical services in the newly emerging office buildings. Now once again the urban environment will be reinvented. Businesses that had housed office workers in tall concrete and glass skyscrapers will move most of those employees out of offices to work remotely at home.**

The radical impact of employees performing as "remote workers" will be far reaching and basically serve to reinvent the city once again. This shift will be perhaps the most important economic impact arising from the Covid-19 Pandemic. One example was that office rents began falling in large cities. The lack of demand for office space will eventually result in some high-rise office buildings eventually retrofitted for other purposes. For example, one might imagine a building consisting of restaurants, salons, and stores, along with limited office and conference areas, where each space is available for rent by the day or even hour for meetings. This is a trend that already started in California during the dot.com boom for consultants and small startups. Similarly, other office buildings could be replaced with new structures designed around the new remote work model with space for parking electric vehicles for hybrid workers who only need to come into the city for occasional physical meetings and team events and do not wish to endure a long and complex commute from their new homes in the extended suburbs. The lack of demand for office space may also result in other office buildings being converted into residential space for individuals who like living in urban centers. As is always the case with free markets, some of the repurposing attempts for the existing high-rise offices will fail while others will be successful. However, it will not be long before a number of these huge high-rise office structures take owners and landlords into bankruptcy.

The older cities, such as New York, San Francisco, Boston, and Philadelphia will be some of the first to show the momentum for the transformation to the Post Pandemic economy. An exodus of existing residents from these cities actually began during the second and third quarter of 2020. During the government-forced shut downs, people of all ages realized the amenities of city life were not as crucial as previously thought. Furthermore, amenities were costly in terms of the real expenses of rent, taxes, transportation hassles, and health hazards.

The inhabitants of these large cities learned that catastrophic scenarios, like Covid-19, can happen rapidly. The big city dwellers may have only seen pandemics in movies, but in 2020 they had experienced it in real life. They learned it seriously disrupts your way of life, especially difficult in a big city, and can even end life. The movie versions did not show all the vexing problems of trying to adjust and mitigate. Moreover, people learned that these horrendous deadly viruses spread particularly quickly in large, densely packed cities dependent on mass transit and close living quarters. These realizations are only two of the reasons to move out of large cities. As time goes on, it appears more difficult to maintain a life in the impersonal confines of the large cities.

Younger residents who were required to work from home quickly realize they no longer needed to live in urban regions. Seniors and retirees that had substantial financial resources were also moving out of urban areas. Of course, you could gamble that a new vaccine would protect you, but the data on flu vaccines did not appear particularly encouraging. The exodus began with the Covid-19 Pandemic, but it is unlikely to subside. These retirees are asking themselves if the large, congested cities are worth the gamble, worth the stress, of staying. There are numerous attractive alternatives to living in the big city both in expand suburban areas and in retirement communities in tourist regions. Just as remote work has changed the need for workers to stay in cities the same virtual meeting technology will allow retiree to stay connected to family and friends from distant communities, leisure activities like fishing, or nature walks.

Countering the negative impacts of remote work on urban areas will include benefits such as reduction of commuter traffic at peak travel hours and less pollution. Instead of blocks and blocks of office buildings as deserts devoid of humans on weekends and week nights, one is apt to see a steady stream of people on weekends and into the night time hours. The reduction of commuter travel peaks on mass transit will also reduce the risk of new viruses spreading quickly through mass transit in urban areas. Nevertheless, there will still be constraints in the ability to provide flexibility during a viral outbreak. For example, in high-rise buildings, the elevators cannot provide sufficient social-distancing potential during a viral outbreak. Adding new and larger elevator shafts is often not an option. Similarly, buses and mass transit cars will also make social distancing difficult. Nevertheless, with many people working remotely, the result will have less of an impact if lockdowns are used for future encounters with pandemics.

However, as with the 1918 Flu Pandemic and previous migrations out of urban areas, the outflow will be countered by inflow of immigrants from overseas who are generally attracted to urban areas. The population of these first-generation immigrants will continue the tradition of large urban areas being culturally "international". That said, the problem for new immigrants will be finding jobs as the office work force goes online and the need for associated ancillary workers will diminish further.

The reductions of office jobs are related to the major urban changes. In the past, support tasks for these office workers drove the urban job opportunities for immigrants. The new immigrant population will be just one of many challenges to reinvent the role of cities in the era following the Covid Shock.

## Rural Development

As we see, rural regions will also change in multifaceted ways because of the Covid-19 Pandemic. The availability of high-speed Internet, expansion of domestic tourism, remote work, agriculture automation, Controlled Environment Agriculture (CEA) and the on-shoring of manufacturing all have the potential to transform the nation's rural economies. Together these Post Pandemic trends are likely to bring a renaissance to rural America.

One of the big game changers for rural America will be the push to bring high-speed Internet to rural parts of the nation. The dependence of economic trends such as remote work and virtual meetings on reliable high-speed Internet was highlighted by the Covid Pandemic. Efforts to link the various rural areas by high-speed Internet will accelerate as a result of the Pandemic. High-speed Internet will create numerous opportunities for rural America. This will make it easier for individuals in rural areas to work remotely. High-speed Internet will also create opportunities for populations in rural areas to find remote work that pays well and allows them to remain in their communities. Individuals can create incomes from online niche retail sites, either independent ones or ones associated with ecommerce retail networks such as Amazon or eBay. The low cost of rural real estate will provide these niche retailers the competitive edge to survive in the new online economy.

The availability of high-speed Internet and alternative energy systems will also make rural areas even more attractive to host Internet *server farms* (the depositories of computers that store data for the Internet). The shift to remote work and virtual meetings will greatly increase the demand for these ancillary facilities. Businesses to support and develop these *server farms* will also be attracted to rural areas.

Rural areas that have economies built on tourism will be impacted by the increased reluctance of individuals to travel internationally, combined with the increase health restrictions on international travel. Local travel will be more desirable for these individuals for vacations and will create a boom in domestic tourism. To reach a destination via a short domestic flight or in the safe isolation of an automobile or RV office will be attractive and compelling options for travel in the Post Pandemic Economy.

The availability of high-speed Internet will also enable remote workers to take extended vacations. Instead of spending only a few days at a tourist destination, they will now be able to spend a month or more while continuing to work remotely. It may well become a trend for individuals interested in a sport like snow skiing to move to the snowy destination of their choice for the entire season instead of the occasional weekend or holiday. If people are into hiking or fly fishing, they may similarly move to a tourist destination to engage in such recreation full time. This wave of semi-permanent tourists could transform many tourist destinations.

Many such tourist destinations may also become locations where remote workers wish to live permanently. Although most remote workers are likely to stay within easy driving distance of urban areas, there is a segment that is looking to move far beyond. No longer tied to an office in urban areas, remote workers will realize they can live wherever they so desire. A trend that began with remote workers moving to rural tourist communities will likely accelerate as the number of remote workers increases Post Pandemic. Retirees leaving urban areas may also want to live in rural communities as we have said. Already "snowbirds" travel from northern urban areas to southern rural communities to avoid harsh winters. The challenges of the Covid-19 Pandemic may well encourage them to become permanent residents.

The automation of agriculture combined with the shortening of supply chains will transform many rural communities. The difficulty of finding farm workers, especially for harvest season, will motivate farmers to adopt more automated technology, switching to crops that are less dependent on harvest workers. Just as robotic technology is transforming manufacturing, robotics will transform agriculture.

Drones are increasingly used today to collect data on farms and ranches while being used to apply pesticides, fertilizer and sowing seeds. Robots are also being developed to harvest fruits and vegetables. Robotic tractors will not need human drivers to operate. The enclosed environment on farms makes them an ideal environment for robotic systems. Often combined with AI these systems are now reducing the labor requirements needed in agriculture. The trends existing before the Covid-19 Pandemic will accelerate in the Post Pandemic Economy.

Another technology platform destined to transform agriculture is Controlled Environment Agriculture (CEA), also called Vertical Farming. CEA is the bringing of high value agricultural crops indoors where the environment is controlled to produce fruits, vegetables, herbs, and flowers year-round for local markets. Land that once had limited access to water could through recycling become extremely productive since CEA greatly reduces the amount of water required to grow a crop. With CEA, farmers stagger the planting so there is continuous production of the crop, eliminating the peaks in labor required in conventionally produced crops. It also allows crops that are traditionally grown in tropical climates to be produced in temperate climates while the controlled environment is ideally suited for robotic systems using AI to optimize yield per acre.

Because CEA is far less dependent on the external environment than traditional agriculture, it could allow a larger variety of locally produced fruits and vegetables to be available in urban areas. The shorter distance the produce needs to travel and the continual harvesting means it will arrive at markets fresher than conventionally produced crops. Since CEA also eliminates the need for pesticides, it allows fruits and vegetables to be grown organically. The desire of individuals for healthier local produce following the Pandemic could provide the market pull needed to transform rural economies.

The switch by industry to shorten supply chains by bringing manufacturing back on shore to the United States, especially for critical goods like medical supplies, has the potential to boost rural economies. Rural communities will make excellent candidate sites for the new factories that will be required to shorten the supply chains for critical goods like medical supplies and pharmaceuticals. Inexpensive land, access to alternative energy, less strict zoning requirements and a workforce with a strong work ethic make rural attract for new facilities. Rural sites are also advantageous in allowing production to continue when future pandemics result in urban lockdowns. The ability of high-speed Internet and access to interstate highways will make rural locations attractive sites for this new Post Pandemic manufacturing boom. Government programs for domestic production of critical medical goods to ensure national security are likely to benefit rural economies.

The Post Pandemic Economy will undoubtedly transform the American landscape over the next decade. The migration of remote workers to suburbs and rural communities will transform their character and better integrate them into the national economy. Cities, as cities do, will reinvent themselves as the demand for office space declines. The changes in travel patterns will change the character of tourism and the hospitality industry. The result will be a whole new tapestry of demographic and geographic patterns that reinvents America.

## Implications

As people migrate from urban areas, they will sell their houses or condos and the science of Economics points to the outcome. As housing units become empty and the number of units up for sale increases, relatively lower prices develop, the demographics of neighborhoods change, resulting in a decline in city tax revenues and public services. Flint, Michigan, following the exodus of the automobile industry is a classic, if extreme, example of this cycle of decline.

However, as with all the other transformations brought about by the necessity to adjust habits, these changes also present us with dynamic new opportunities. It is wise for you and all of us to consider this new Post Covid-19 Pandemic landscape switching careers, making new investments, moving, adopting new technologies and other innovative alternatives that increase wealth, enhance lifestyles or provide new benefits.

The methods and approach for making lifestyle altering decisions after the Covid Shock we identify and discuss in the last chapter of this book.

# CHAPTER 9

## Understanding the Economics behind the Big Picture

### Economic Forces

The substitution of remote workers for office workers, the substitution of AI Robotics for human workers, the repurposing of factories, office buildings and other structures arise from the actions of suppliers and consumers in the competitive marketplace. Effective business managers look to "outdo" the competition by producing more efficiently, respecting the safe environments for employees, and producing products that better satisfy their customers. The complex economic process was explained in simple common-sense terms by Professor Adam Smith, the "Father of Economics" who described the functions of individual self-interest and competition 244 years ago in his book titled *An Inquiry into the Nature and Causes of the Wealth of Nations.* Professor Smith showed how the combination of *individual self-interest and competition* would provide an economic outcome offering the highest productivity for the greatest number of people. Smith poetically referred to this process as "an invisible hand" guiding a national free-market economy to the best outcome.

Smith's analysis endures as the foundation for understanding how free-market economies operate as opposed to government-planned economies that employ government "experts" to make decisions related to production and distribution. In fact, most of the economic activity we see around us today is the result of self-interested behavior within markets. Adam Smith's lengthy book of two volumes (some 1,000 pages, published in 1776) contained detailed explanations of the free-market mechanisms that produce *The Wealth of Nations*. Note one of the hundreds of insightful statements in his book:

> "It is not from the benevolence of the butcher, the brewer, or the baker that we expect our dinner, but from their regard to their own interest."

Indeed, all producers and sellers of products and services expect their incomes not from the benevolence of their customers, but from customers' self-interest in purchasing the products or services. Likewise, the sellers' self-interest is to make sure that patrons are satisfied with the purchases. Therefore, it is not a rivalry where others' needs and desires are ignored. Instead, the seller's product and his service must satisfy the patrons, otherwise buyers will go elsewhere (competition in the markets). Smith described how individual behavior in a *competitive market*-oriented economy results in not only satisfying individual interests, but also promotes the overall public interests better than otherwise (better than any other type of system). For example, regarding the producer/seller working in a market based economy, Professor Smith wrote:

> "By directing that industry in such a manner as its produce may be of the greatest value, he intends only his own gain, and he is in this, as in many other cases, led by an *invisible hand* to promote an end which was no part of his intention. By pursuing his own interest, he frequently promotes that of the society more effectually than when he really intends to promote it. I have never known much good done by those who affected to trade for the public good."

Overall, this market-based system of open competition through self-interest maximizes the aggregate material wellbeing of both suppliers and customers in the market, and therefore *renders the highest material wellbeing to the nation's citizens* (mathematically provable).

Furthermore, we know that everyone is necessarily a "consumer" in any society or economy. In addition, adults are frequently also employed in a business, which is owned either by them or by someone else (otherwise they are unemployed or retired workers, but still consumers). It does not matter whether activity is said to be *for-profit* or *not-for-profit*, because today everything *except the operations of government* is a type of business, due to the absolute requirement that in a private market economy total revenues must be at least as much as expenditures, otherwise the organization experiences inability to continue operations (bankruptcy and termination). Some people fail to recognize this irrefutable truth. Nothing is produced and delivered without costs (i.e., no product or service can be "free" of the expenses to produce and deliver).

For example, some people might counter argue that the local religious organization is not a business. However, it is an inescapable reality that the Churches, Synagogues or other religious institutions must take in sufficient revenues to cover the expenses of the buildings, electric utilities, transportation, interest on financial borrowings, and the payments for support of the pastors, priests, rabbis, and employees, etc. Whatever services the religious organizations provide, the organizations are not without expenses to produce and deliver. Likewise, state or local government must also have sufficient revenues to cover expenditures or they also will eventually experience a debt so large as to force bankruptcy, resulting in collapse of state or local government services or default on its interest-bearing bonds.

Essentially, in a Market Economy every entity is a business of some type. The problem is that state or local government office holders know that it is easier to borrow more money than to raise taxes, so they raise taxes where they can and borrow profusely by issuing bonds. The political office holders also know that their term of "service" could end before the government is totally ruined by the burdensome debt. A government organization is inefficient because the official authorities dictate the product or service and taxes (price of services) without competition during their terms in office. The transaction is not determined synchronously (happening at the same time) with respect to public bargaining in a competitive market.

The politicians know that they can probably be reelected by simply promising voters new and marvelous policies, which when carried out will provide the voters new and more benefits. Unlike incomes of business owners and managers, the politicians' incomes are not linked to the costs of their programs that they impose on the government treasury and unavoidably the tax paying public. Therefore, unlike the people working in a competitive market-based economy of private ownership, the politicians do not need to operate the most efficient, effective and resilient management practices.

The political legislators do not fund their programs with their personal financial investments. Moreover, in an open Market economy, all prices and costs are determined by the buyers and sellers in competition without government officials dictating production and distribution. This explains why and how the private market process is superior to any government planned economy.

Most everyone is aware of the possibility for false advertising and deceptive marketing by company managers. What the government office holders can and should do is make sure that the citizens are aware of any industries operating via corruption, cheating, lying, or embezzling. Government can provide for transparency in the private market economic system without causing problems for open market production and distribution built on honest ethical principles for performance.

With the government ensuring honest transparency for business enterprise, the management of businesses will avoid chicanery because they know they cannot run such practices without consumers' ultimate awareness. Therefore, business management will avoid chicanery because integrity is in a business owner's self-interest. It is once again a fundamental aspect of self-interest creating the best outcome for all concerned. One important caveat may be that government officials are not known for their own transparency, and can commit political chicanery. Therefore whenever discovered, these government authorities need to be summarily exposed and removed, it goes without saying.

The market economy with its natural incentives for innovation and competition for customers provides the maximum benefit for producers and customers alike, and is therefore provides the best economic system. A free-market based system is in constant search for the best solutions for satisfying consumers, no government planned top-down system for production and distribution can match this level of performance. The alternative is government planned and operated economy, essentially the same as operating every as a monopoly because there is no competition to incentivize innovation, no real incentive to search for a means to lower costs and prices. In a government planned economy, there are no free market prices to signal the production and distribution according to the individual consumers' valuation of products and services. Therefore, government planners and technocrats lack this crucial information only an open market economy can create and hence utilize.

Governments can be useful in preventing monopolies from developing in private enterprise, but the government itself should not prevent honest free-market competitive activities by creating a government owned and operated monopoly itself. The only exceptions are a few things in which the market mechanism cannot efficiently provide. A national highway system of roads is one example. The characteristic that distinguishes a "pure public product or service" from a purely private product or service is that **one person's use does not diminish the ability of someone else to use the same product or service simultaneously**. Your consumption does not exclude someone else's consumption. In other words, traditional Supply and Demand activity in a market cannot correctly identify how much of a highway system to build and maintain. This is a public item that must be left for the government. However, because in government there are ***no consumer market determined prices*** there is no perfect data to signal the exact amount to produce. This is why governments have been known to build the infamous highways to nowhere.

Credit: Pexels – Jan Kroon

Even if you consider the idea of a privately-owned toll road highway system, it would be impractical for satisfying the national economic need. Similarly, another public item is National Defense because it cannot be a private service, Private Supply and Demand activity in a market does not correctly identify precisely how much of a military defense a nation needs to build and therefore maintain.

Nevertheless, unlike highways and military, most of the products and services a society wants are optimally provided through the private market system enlisting the individual incentives of producers, buyers and sellers.

## Human Behavior and Analytics of Economics

In the preceding chapters of this book, we have presented the behavioral changes associated with the disruptions caused by the Covid-19 Pandemic, and we arrived at the implications for the Post-Covid "New Normal" way of life.

The major systematic functions and principles of human behavior are disclosed by the science of Economics, and its basic principles and interactions. In the preceding chapter, we presented the fundamental principles. Much of the science of economics has advanced in many ways since the $18^{th}$ century of Professor Adam Smith and his book *An Inquiry into Nature and Causes of the Wealth of Nations,* but the fundamental principles Professor Smith identified still apply. During the two and a half centuries since Adam

Smith's pioneering how economies work and what forces exist within all economies it has been elevated to a true science. Contemporary Economic analysis now uses the same tools that are employed in the physical sciences such as Physics, Chemistry and Biology. Modern Economics uses the highest levels of mathematics and statistical analysis. However, long-term forecasts are improbable because of the existence of two entities and their cooperative arrangement.

The *first entity* is the "heavy hand" of the bankers bank (the central bank). In the USA, the central bank is not an agency of the Federal government, despite the fact that the name of the corporation is the "Federal Reserve Bank" often referred to as "The Fed." Instead of being a government agency, it is owned by the member banks, operated and overseen by an elected board of bankers. This central bank controls the issue of the U.S. dollar. Essentially, it can imagine any amount of dollars into existence, and claim this amount as its official "dollar reserves" in its account. There is no physical anchor to identify the value of the unit of a dollar, because after 1971, gold and silver were removed as backing of currency. Therefore, after 1971, new Reserves are simply imagined into existence by the controllers of the central bank. The *second entity* is the U.S. government's net expenditures beyond taxes received. This excess spending becomes the Federal government's issue of new Treasury Bonds for sale, and buyers are mostly the banks. The central reserve bankers' bank would never refuse to purchase the government's excessive debt because of the fear of losing its special franchise to operate. Consequently, there is no formula or set of equations precisely forecast long-term future changes in the "Money Supply" or future changes in "Government Expenditures." Because there is no fixed anchor to restrict issuance of imaginary money, and secondly the U.S. Congress spending decisions are political, Economics cannot offer irrefutable quantitative long-range forecasts.

Nevertheless, we are learning more about some of the thought processes that rest behind the known relationship of human behavioral actions and reactions. Many of these relationships are determined by new knowledge concerning the process of human deliberations, a function of the brain. Therefore, we will briefly look at what is known about cognition and why people arrive at alternative behaviors and habits. In other words, how and why a segment of humanity can arrive at a variety of decisions. As previously mentioned, much of society's mutations over time can be identified by fundamental principles of Economics. An economy is a system affected by *external events* such as pandemics, but *external events* are independently evaluated by the internal process of each person's thinking. The thought process of each person has alternative pathways, identified as follows:

1) Opinions from Beliefs
2) Identity thought and defense
3) Fantasy
4) Unbiased conclusions from the scientific method.

Human beings behave disparately depending upon use of one or another of neural paths.

**Opinions are most often loosely formed and quickly uttered responses. Opinions are weak conclusions arising from limited reasoning and/or involving limited information. Everyone has some opinions because no one is capable of actually knowing "everything." However, opinions have no real value, except as a possible early starting point for a subsequent more serious examination in order to discover truth.** For example, opinions can be restated as *testable hypotheses*, and then be mathematically tested for logical consistency, and next statistically tested with probability techniques using a set of plenary data. **This is the basis of "scientific method."**

By application of the scientific method, the conclusion may reveal reality (truth). There are two aspects to the testing for reality: 1) for logical integrity; and 2) for degree of authenticity using statistical techniques of analytics on evidence (data). Thus, the conclusion drawn from the testing process will result in a measure of statistical probability, *which provides a numerical measure for the inference, in other words, for the degree of reliability of the consequence of the hypothesis.* An extremely high probability grants confidence in terms of reality (truth). This is the method and these are the techniques that separate Science from mere conjecture, and untested opinions, which have not been subjected to rigorous analytical discovery.

An interesting observation is that many of the opinions that people holdup as "truth" are not only held without examining them properly, but these opinions are most often not even formulated by the person. **Most people hold opinions that they simply borrowed from other people. The more that someone borrows opinions, the less they really know.** You may have encountered people that will say, *"It is my personal truth and I do not agree with you."* **When a person takes that position, there can be no further discussion, investigation or debate.** Moreover, the idea of "personal truth" is the same as saying *"It is my personal reality."* That is nonsensical because we all live on the same plane of existence, that of actual reality. Moreover, reality does not care about people's illusions. Reality simply exists. What we may not "like," for any reason, does not change the fundamental laws of physics or economics.

> *"Sometimes people do not want to hear the truth because they do not want to have their illusions destroyed."* Friedrich Nietzsche

Likewise, people harbor **beliefs**. These may be founded in recognition of reality (truth) or they may be a conjecture and not scientifically tested for ultimate validity. As an example, consider a small child, the toddler, a little girl or boy startled by a strange animal that appears hostile. The animal could be a dog baring its teeth or barking because it is fearful of the little person. The child concludes that this type of animal is very dangerous and must always be avoided. If the animal is a small pet, such as a dog, the person when as an adult may have a fear of all dogs. Many people who formed false beliefs from early experiences carried the belief for the remainder of their lives.

> *"In the long run, the most unpleasant truth is a safer companion that a pleasant falsehood."* Theodore Roosevelt

Harboring falsehoods is unfortunate, but not uncommon. Furthermore, certain biological forces work against pure logical thought processes. The unseen forces of genetic inheritance and hormones that result in "feelings" are working in a manner to **modify otherwise purely logical reasoning.** The brain selects certain aspects of evidence on which to focus attention. Recent research indicates the human brain has a high degree of selectivity in processing information. Evidence proves individuals identified as "optimistic thinkers" largely reject negative information, thereby allowing them to maintain a positive view of the world.

Humanity will always nurse contrary personal opinions, creating endless conflict because we are biologically determined to behave in such a mode. Does that conclusion shock you? Consider all the history of the past several thousand years. Scientists reveal to us that conflict appears to be buried deep within the brain's scaffolding, particularly within the male gender of the species (and perhaps the males of other animal species as well). Nevertheless, most females can contribute to conflict because they identify with the same male survival instincts, thereby explaining why females frequently select their associations with conflict-winning males.

Consequently, the often seemingly outrageous positions of differing groups are "normal" in the sense they share common biological behaviors. It appears that cross-cultural hostilities also have biological foundation, which is built into the nature of humanity. Whether the group is one with which we argue or one with which we identify, it is partly a physical process of nature at work. For example, there will always be "conservatives" and "liberals" in societies, and these polarities will continue in opposition since they are the result of human genetic physical composition. University of Virginia psychologist Dr. Jonathan Haidt, a researcher on the evolutionary psychology of morality says, **"Our righteous minds are designed by evolution to unite us into teams, divide us against other teams, and blind us to the truth."**

This explains why debates and arguments between groups rarely convert a member of the opposition.

Evolutionary biologists maintain that natural selection has bestowed an array of ancestral genes, brain processes, and hormonal systems to help us accomplish complex decision-making, but it also dictates the forming of strong alliances within groups that are necessarily in opposition.

The decidedly social nature of the species rewards people who ally themselves in tightly knit groups, and such groups will exhibit "brotherhood" or "sisterhood." These affiliations in turn allow us to accomplish collectively what an individual alone cannot, whether it is primitive man hunting in groups or tribes of men at war or business strategies of management in competitive commerce. This mentality is exhibited in a variety of ways: today we see group identity and behavior of sports fans demonstrating for a particular team, religious groups fighting over moral superiority, political party affiliation, corporate competitions for market dominance, and the need for militaries.

The most popular computer games are based in tribal conflict (most frequently illustrated environments depict either historical or mythical or modern warfare). Such universal popularity is not accidental. We appear to be biologically engineered to see the world from the perspective of groups with which we identify. Furthermore, it is not simply the members of opposing groups who are deeply affected by emotions, which can thwart purely logical reasoning; it is the *nature of humanity in all groups*.

Many people prefer to think that our positions and behaviors are determined by pure mechanical reason alone. However, the process of reasoning is embedded in a bath of hormones inside our brains, and strongly impelled by biological genetic inheritance, along with frequently borrowed opinions from other people, group customs, and reinforced by habits that are gained from repetition. **Habits, doing the same thing over and over, we recognize as commonplace. However, when society encounters catastrophic disruptions, habits change accordingly. Such is the transition into the new era following the Covid Shock.**

Until the Covid-19 Pandemic, the top ten leading causes of death in the USA remained consistent, but the 2020 death statistics vary significantly. With over 300,000 Covid related deaths by end of 2020 and projected to rise to 500,000 by the end of January 2021, and many more thousands of deaths later into 2021, Covid-19 would be the third most common cause of death on the list of top-10 causes.

The top-10 leading causes of death accounted for nearly three-quarters of all deaths. Heart disease and cancer remained on top of the list with 1,254,000 deaths. These top-2 leading causes were greater than all the other causes by a large margin. Accidents were previously the third leading cause and showing, only about 166,000 deaths. In the United States, the 2020 population was estimated at 331,002,651 people at midyear according to UN data. Those over 70 years of age were approximately 47.9 million, and count in the age range of people with a higher susceptibility to serious complications from the virus.

More specifically, the Center for Disease Control and Prevention (CDC.gov) stated, *"The greatest risk for severe illness from COVID-19 is among those aged 85 or older."* The total number of people in the USA that was 85 or older was estimated at 6.5 million (less than .0195 percent of total population). However, not all contract the virus and not all die, so the *overall* U.S. mortality rate is relatively very low.

**Actual deaths** of those with Covid-19 in this population segment were around thirty-three thousand or **0.0050 percent of the 6.5 million people age 85 or above.** However, most of the population was unaware of the low probability of death from the Covid-19 virus.

Moreover, public officials wanted to exercise an abundance of caution. Therefore, most states in the USA closed schools, and instituted serious restrictions. The major media promoted the idea of children wearing masks whenever they left home. Some people wondered if closing all the schools was really warranted.

Nevertheless, the general political and media narrative supported shutdowns of the economy, and other restrictions on daily life that appear contrary to the actual significance of the statistics. The theme of most media narratives gave the impression that everyone is exceedingly vulnerable. It is no wonder that the public was extremely fearful of any social interactions of any type. Examining the government's CDC data, as published in December 2020 of *The Economist* provides a more realistic perspective.

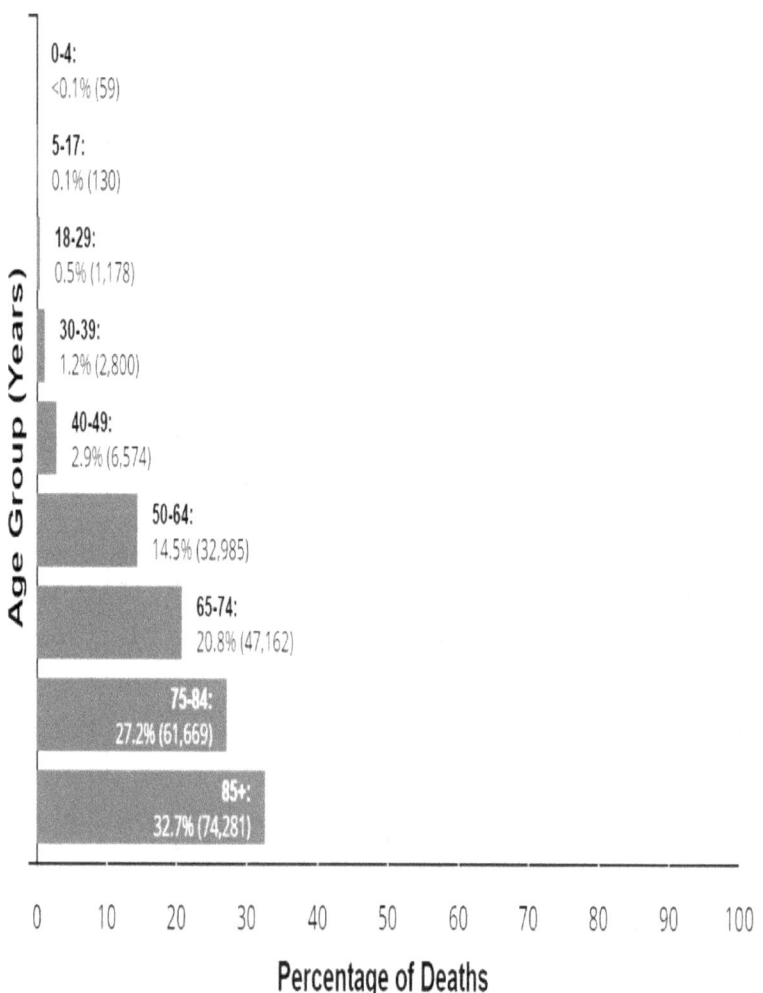

The data for School age children showed a one-tenth of one percent death rate from Covid (0.1%). Young adults age 18 to 29 showed a 1.17% rate reported as Covid deaths. Older adults 30 to 39 showed 1.2%. Seniors, age 75 to 84 showed 27.2%, and the highest percentage was reported to be 32.7% for ages over 85 years.

After the Covid-19 Pandemic, when an entire public becomes generally aware of this information, how will the public process the information? The question of how the public will react in the future is critical for the economy. Currently we can know how people's habits changed, and we can forecast the impact, but what specific habits may be temporary and not produce long-term changes? This is the question of known and unknowns. In other words, we know the influence of opinions, beliefs and some biological differences, as we consider the historical data of previous pandemics.

Unbiased scientific reasoning is a very difficult task, and most scholarly Economists attempt to do it consistently, but are not always successful. We know that in the general population, most people exhibit a predisposition toward group thought and behavior; they do not always use pure reason and do not utilize the totality of the evidence available. Instead, they select data that is limited evidence, but may appear to support their **opinions within their group identity**.

However, the most common decisions involved in activities of *commerce* are rational and are displayed consistently. Economics has been successful in identifying the interrelationships and consequences of these behaviors. The science of Economics has revealed how external factors affect the production and purchasing of products and services. The consistency of market behaviors is remarkable.

## Conclusion

The body of knowledge in Economics is branch of learning that can disclose producers' behavior and consumers' behavior when there is an exogenous change. There are "laws of Economics" (much like "the laws of Physics"). These axioms point to the way that people will react to experiences, in this case the reactive behaviors to the experiences of the Covid-19 Pandemic. These predictable reactions are the pathway to the Post-Covid Great Economic Transition.

Humans form groups for cooperating to compete with others; they adapt, innovate, and implement new practices and thereby maintain the economic benefits of society. Economic analysis, properly applied, is science and not merely the "art of opinion". It can elucidate the way toward the Post Pandemic Economy. Knowing the "Laws of Economics" can help individuals to consider the most probable changes in their society and culture.

Economic analysis accurately considered, can lead the way a person to reap benefits from the new opportunities in the Post Pandemic Economy. In order to accomplish this objective, you need to plan, design your life choices, and travel the best route to reach your new destination.

Planning your journey is described in the next chapter.

# CHAPTER 10

## How to create your Plan for the Post Pandemic Economy

The "Old Normal" is gone, the "New Normal" is underway, and evolving in the manner that we have described in the previous chapters. Readers have learned about new opportunities and the benefits. Therefore, you may want to plan for seizing upon the best opportunities. Unquestionably, it is important to acknowledge this aim before we discuss how to create your plan, and it may be helpful if we reconsider some of the strategies. Meanwhile, we shall list many of the "Winners" and "Losers" of "The Great Economic Transition."

## Winners in the Post Pandemic Economy

- Individuals who are well trained and practiced in remote work

- Businesses that adopt remote work
- Office supply stores with curbside/delivery that support remote work
- Restaurants with take out, delivery or drive through
- Low density suburban areas more than 45 minutes from dense urban areas
- Vacation communities and destinations attractive to remote workers
- RV dealers and manufacturers that supply the vehicles for remote workers to tour the nation
- Domestic tourism services
- Home improvement businesses serving remote workers that spend money they save from not commuting and invest it upgrading their homes
- Gardening centers
- Online retailers with rapid delivery services
- Facilities that provide shared offices/conference rooms for occasional meetings
- Suppliers of personal recreation equipment such as bicycles, running shoes, etc.
- Video streaming services
- Churches and Synagogues
- Mobile high-speed Internet providers

- Online video gaming
- Providers of domestic manufactured medical supplies and personal protection equipment
- Home gym equipment suppliers
- Movers, moving companies, and truck rental businesses

## Losers in the Post Pandemic Economy

- Urban transit systems
- Businesses dependent on urban office building clusters
- Owners of large office buildings
- Firms that reject remote work
- Automobile manufacturers that do not or cannot rebalance their offering of new vehicles. Moreover, since the remote workers drive their cars less, they will not need to replace their vehicles as often.
- Suppliers of gasoline and other auto services as remote workers drive their cars less
- Workout Gyms, since many people have chosen to create a "home gym"
- Theaters, as fewer people gather in very large social settings

- Restaurants that only allow in-house dining
- Cruise lines
- International tourism
- Airlines
- Airliner manufacturers
- High tax areas since the remote workers will move out and relocate

## Trends and Chain Reactions

The list of Winners and Losers is not exhaustive but suggests the chain reaction of accelerating trends as the work environment progressively changes and the Post Pandemic Economy evolves.

Transformations affecting diverse industries have been discussed throughout this book. Examine the implications. With the arrival of the "New Normal", life can be enhanced, if you make wise choices. Identify the axis of happiness for yourself in the "New Normal."

In all things Post Covid Shock, you need to identify which aspects affect you the most, whether in a positive manner or a negative one. Then you will know how to chart your path successfully for the "New Normal."

## Consider moving out and moving on

If you are or will be a Remote Worker, location is one of your most important choices. If you are living in a big city, you do not have to remain. The big city and its downtown is an urban hassle, costly and often such cities are deteriorating. You have options. You can literally live anywhere the Internet reaches. In the USA that is just about everywhere in the country. Your choices are abundant. Study them carefully.

1. Investigate the locales in terms of amenities, cost of living and taxes.

2. The compensation question is an important factor in your overall analysis. Employers have always based salaries on location. Some employers are planning to base remote work-at-home employee compensation on the employee's home location, which means employees moving from a higher -cost-of-living areas to a less expensive one may be faced with reduced salaries. If your current net-debt is low, then this might not affect your choice because the new cost of living will be low enough to balance the net reduced income effect and is marginal.

3. Examine the public services in terms quality. Are public services in decline?

4. Examine the challenges and requirements of moving, such as selling your city unit, or getting out of a lease or subletting if it is an option.

You will likely be surprised by the differences and advantages of relocating. Even if you decide against a move, your investigation allows you to make an informed decision. It eliminates guessing and suffering from the anxiety of uncertainty.

Remember, the first wave of people moving out of big cities has already transpired. There are more waves to come. At some later date, many opportunities will have been seized by people seeking these advantages. Those individuals who make changes early frequently have a competitive advantage in securing a larger reward.

## Retirement implications

What if you are close to the age for retirement? This is a prime season of your life to think about location for retirement. It could be that your location choice for retirement is already a match with your remote work location. Imagine how fortuitous that may be. Less stress, more fun and you could arrive sooner.

## Hybrid Work Locations

Even if your occupation does not afford you the choice of working entirely remote using online communications but now a "hybrid work environment" that causes you to be in some aspect tied to the city, you need to investigate your options for the best residence. In other words, you mostly work from home, but occasionally are required to be in the big city. If that applies to you, then suburbs and other nearby locations may offer you a better lifestyle.

Your analysis for decision making requires a system for data entry and options. The options can be depicted in a "decision tree". Here you can use a system called Decision Mapping, creating and applying a map to your decision tree and entering the results of your investigation.

Making an informed decision means first considering a range of options. Each has advantages and disadvantages. Moreover, these options have supporting evidence to empower your planning process.

Decision Mapping displays this complex process of "thinking about the options," showing the process of deliberation within a diagram. When a person constructs a Decision Map (DM), it is more than mere imagery; it is a visualization that connects possible interactions and the "branches" like crossroads that depict the different pathways (routes) to goals and objectives.

You need a realistic rendering of your Decision Map. Label the pathways that show alternative routes. Your Decision Map is like a roadmap where not all roads may lead to the same terminus. As your Decision Map develops, you will note differences between one path and another.

Mapping information, and what it implies, is a graphical representation of the process of thinking about options. In this case, it is helpful for at least two reasons:

1. The activity of creating a map helps you to state the options and evidence cogently, clearly, succinctly and tangibly.

2. A decision map is physical and enduring tool whenever you consult it. Making decisions for the "New Normal" requires time to investigate and time to reflect. Constructing your DM may require several days. Every time you return to thinking about a problem of choice, you may forget something, but the map does not. It is like having a shopping list with you that helps you make your purchase decisions.

Credit: Pexel - Christina Morello

If you are unfamiliar with the activity of Decision Mapping, there are numerous articles and lessons freely available on the Internet.

## Economic changes come in Waves

The first wave of people moving out and moving on has already occurred with more waves to come. Consider the choices whatever your occupation may be or if self-employed, whatever your business enterprise, you may still need to investigate your options and other locations that may offer you a better lifestyle choice. Whether you decide to move or not, there are other considerations.

## Consider Consumer Demand in your Industry

In this book, you learned about the Post Pandemic Economy, and the diversity business and lifestyle. Consider your industry in light of the changes that arise during the Great Economic Transition. How will the changes affect your ability to be productive in the new circumstances?

**For example**, impact of the Covid Shock resulted in various industries encountering severe costs due to the shutdowns. Businesses that survived will adopt some varied methods for operating in the "New Normal." *However, the more important factor is how consumers react going forward.*

Review the changes in customer behavior identified in this book that relate to the industry that concerns you.

1. How do the predicted changes in customer behavior affect your industry?
2. Is the expected change in customer behavior to be long lasting?
3. What do you need to do in order to prepare for these changes?

For instance, the Cruise Industry faces a lowering Demand for their product. The lower Demand can be expected to last for at least a few years. People faced traumatic conditions during the Pandemic, and many now have a lower tolerance for risk taking. Over time, cruising the seas aboard large vessels with thousands of other customers will again be seen as a reasonably safe activity, but it will take years to win back all of the previous consumer Demand for cruising. The industry will not return to the Pre-Pandemic level for a long time.

If you are in this industry or a supplier to the industry, it affects you because the New Normal is not just a return to the pre-Pandemic economy.

## Consider the Changes in Production Methods

Moving into the "New Normal" will incentivize business leaders to invest in the latest technologies. These include upgrading software programs to reduce the need for certain employees. There is also a higher level of interest in Robotics. In the early years of the 21$^{st}$ century, we began to see greater emphasis on intelligent technologies that substitute for the need for human workers. Some are of these technologies are essentially computer software, and others are mechanized constructs that go beyond what was earlier adoption of "automation." Early automation did replace many employees, but it was the type of machinery that still required some line operators. These operators needed a modest upgrade in skills.

Now, with the advances and increasing investment in Artificial Intelligent machines and more elaborate robotic systems integration, the new factory worker's skill set depends on not only on training but the ability to understand how the robotics works. The remaining workers in robotic factories need to be able to do mathematical calculations quickly, read well, write well, and communicate by speaking precisely to their managements.

## More Education or Training

Looking backward in time, we can see that a half century ago, high school graduates in the USA had the foundational skills necessary for most any entry level employment. The public schools ranked near the top in the world. *However*, ***afterward the fundamental***

***standards consistently eroded and the U.S. now ranks near the bottom.*** Businesses wanted better educated employees, and the jobs increasingly went to college educated graduates, as high school graduates were unemployed or working the lowest paid jobs. The change in standards resulted in the problem. Understandably, many of the high school graduates wanted to go to colleges and universities.

The college administrators at most institutions lowered the admission standards to accommodate the increase of applicants. Professors were rewarded for developing new programs, most often with less demanding studies, with little or no discernable pathway to employment after graduation.

For example, there were no productive jobs that actually required a college graduate in "Multiple Gender Studies" or "Philosophy of Relativeness." The number of elective courses proliferated, and previous mandatory courses that were a fundamental and valuable basis for learning were often made voluntary in the curriculum. This allowed students to earn credit units and graduate without having learned the necessary fundamentals. Students "earned" diplomas and graduated without ever taking courses in the basic sciences such as Economics.

Student retention became the goal of most administrators of the campuses across the nation. The faculty was rewarded for "**student retention**," not for failing students that had not earned what had previously been considered a passing grade. The outcome was a bit bothersome; it was called **grade-inflation** where the highest mark of "A" became the norm among students in many universities, including some with the highest ranking. The letter grade of A was essentially equivalent the former average grade of "C" or at most the previous "B" grade. Moreover, for the students that could not reach the standard they receive the new C standard instead of a letter grade of D or F. They simply did not get the D or F of the previous standard. Instead, students could receive the newer revised "C", satisfying the administrators mandate for high levels of "student retention."

These are the primary reasons why the work environments demand additional education and training. The work requirements developing the era following the Covid Shock will require higher educational standards, not only in colleges and universities, but also in the high schools. Most students need at least the basic standards of what was taught a half century ago, before the students graduating can successfully participate in what becomes the New Normal.

The factories that become commonplace will look something like the most forward-looking factories that appeared in the mid-2000s. Examples include the manufacture of vehicles. The automobile and truck production lines significantly change the work environment and fewer employees are required.

Large and somewhat ominous looking robots surround the long production lines and perform the tasks of assembly that were previously done by human workers. The invention, investment and adoption of AI and Robotics will increase during the post Covid Shock era and become the inevitable development of the Great Economic Transformation.

Credit: Pexels – Craig Adderley

In a Factory producing vehicles such as Tesla, people are not needed for assembly on the production line. Robots do the work, significant shift from the previous method of assembly.

Most of the factories, from now forward will be designed for more operations to be done by robotics, and therefore the factories will employ far fewer human beings. Even in the production and assembly of more robots.

## Reviewing Expected Changes likely in Your Occupation

1. Investigate the recent trade publications for information on available and forthcoming technologies in your field of employment.

2. How do the predicted adoptions of various technologies affect the need for your participation in production and servicing?

3. What do you need to do in order to prepare for these changes?

Whatever the industry, there will be increasing investment in new technologies and adoption of robotic methods. This means applications of upgraded and new skills are in demand, whether the robotics are in manufacturing, services, wholesale sales, or retail. Any changes are apt to affect you in some manner.

Nonetheless, we are still a long way from what the science fiction writers have envisioned. They write about a future of sentient AI that does not require human beings to maintain or reproduce the robots, because the robots maintain themselves and reproduce more. At that time, self-knowing and reproducing robotics can be found in all areas of production and distribution.

Artificial Intelligence far exceeds the speed of human ability to calculate. That is one reason why your computer can beat the human Chess Masters. Furthermore, in Chess, there are many possible moves of pieces on the board, but there are not infinite possibilities. That is why AI can beat the human.

However, the human mind occasionally conceives something that does not yet exist, and the nonexistent entity appears unrelated to what is known. Perhaps in the far future of the science fiction writer such human intelligence need not be a factor in a society where no human needs "work." This is an interesting thought, but perhaps of no practical value to anyone living in the 21$^{st}$ Century. Our future is the "New Normal" seeded in the year 2020 during the Covid-19 era, given birth in 2021, fostered, growing and evolving thereafter. This is what you need to contemplate and evaluate your plans for the years following 2021.

## Management and Corporate Culture

We know that the movement of employees from working in offices to working remotely is significant. Furthermore, it is not a temporary change, but a fundamental and long-term shift for a large percentage of employees. Management is responsible for the corporate culture, and critical management paradigms.

A remote workplace culture requires that management continues to support company ideals. Corporate culture represents the behaviors that establish how an organization's employees interact and how they perform jobs. Fundamentally, a workplace culture supports and motivates workers' best efforts to be productive, to feel proud to be associated with the company, and to find a sense of fulfillment in their jobs. Remote work does *not* have to change the values of the culture, but it does need to change the way management contributes to the goals. Therefore, companies through their managers need to establish aspects of *the virtual environment* that satisfy all the characteristics of the original corporate culture. In this manner, all the employees will feel aligned within the usual company structure.

A study surveying remote workers revealed the three most critical components of creating a strong virtual office culture are:

- Virtual workshops with continued learning opportunities (68%)
- Weekly staff meetings and one-on-ones with managers (66%)
- Schedule flexibility (65%)

There are simple ways to translate the valuable activities previously done in offices to be accomplished in remote distanced settings.

1. First, executives and managers need to *review the activities and behaviors that supported the corporate culture* when everyone was in the same building complex. For example, prior to remote work environments, management may have had regular weekly meetings in informal settings with employees. Perhaps, once a week it was a team lunch. This can be simulated by holding a synchronous virtual luncheon meeting. The screen will probably be filled with the employees sipping their favorite drinks (coffee continues to be number one). However, the meeting should not be long. In fact, it is possible to use many of the successful culture building methods in virtual environments.

2. Second, because people are not all gathered together in the same place and at the same time, management must be *careful not to depreciate the need of remote workers to set their own routines*.

3. With everyone working from different locations and personal work schedules, there may be more required for management to keep track of things that could be overlooked and go undone.

4. Management establishes *communication norms of best practices* to ensure clarity, including

response time frames for phone conversations or online chats, and email etiquette. Setting communication standards prevents employees from getting barraged with messages, having their work interrupted and losing focus. The standards should rarely need to be changed because stable standards make communication easier for everyone.

5. Most managers avoid being a "micro-manager" hovering over employees instead of guiding them. At first, the move to managing remote workers was probably somewhat taxing because it was new and very different. Some managers experience anxiety and worry excessively. Remote workers have autonomy. They have some independence and are self-sufficient. A manager cannot simply walk up to the employee and make comments or some swift observation. That is not a big loss, and the autonomy of remote work need not disrupt the prime core values of the company's culture. Management needs to avoid becoming a work disruption or developing a tendency to micromanage.

With experience, remote management and maintaining the core values of the corporate culture becomes easier than expected.

6. Management needs to realize that there is an advantage for the remote worker to have control of their work environment. The remote worker's

control is one of the most important reasons that remote workers can be more productive because they are often *better able to focus on their work without the distractions* arising from other people stopping by their desk, making noise, or even simply walking around in an office environment.

7. The virtual platforms offer opportunities for similar interpersonal communications and teamwork if used judiciously.

8. Management can give equipment to remote employees. In addition, offering corporate objects with company symbols can carry reminders of comradery and pride in the corporate culture.

Businesses have mottos, missions, goals, and employees can identify with the pride in which these are displayed. The corporate coffee cup is an old example. Now, the old is new because it can be the corporate cup at home. The company can also order gourmet coffees and teas to be delivered to the remote employees. Some reflection on how the values and goals of a company were communicated and reinforced before employees became distant remote workers, will eventually inspire management to lead the way.

# Regarding Investments

The economic perspectives explored in this book may help individuals in business and investing in the economy following the Covid Shock.

However, the authors make no claims for the book to advise on particular investments. We are professional Economic scholars, but not licensed by any government authority as personal fiduciaries or advisors for stock market investments and trading in such markets. Nor are the authors licensed by government authority for real estate investment transactions. If you are an experienced investor in these markets, you already have various informational sources and analytical tools and techniques for assisting you in decision making, and you will decide your own activity, making your choices for investments with or without the recommendation of professional market advisors or other trusted sources, as you determine and assume the responsibility accordingly. Similarly, if you are inexperienced in these markets, but plan to make investments, obtaining serious training should be your priority. Otherwise, your search for exploiting investment opportunities in the new and developing economy might be futile and costly.

## When will the Coronavirus go away?

Is it possible to eradicate the SARS-CoV-2 novel coronavirus? Is expecting a zero-Covid world a realistic future?

The best answer comes from the studied expectation of scientists; most agree that Covid-19 will become endemic for the future with more variants developing over time. Periodic waves of the virus and its variants will occur regularly like the influenza virus. The authors of this book foresee 10 impacts of the virus as possibly endemic.

1. First, it reinforces the shift to remote work, already more than 20% of the total workforce is likely to be remote after the Pandemic panic diminishes, with many of these remote workers being in fields that have required a college degree. This number will be even higher if predictions are correct and the virus becomes endemic. This means that businesses that require their workers to return to the office, or even using a hybrid model, will have competitive pressure to allow many employees to continue working remotely.

2. Second, because workers who are fully remote may work from anywhere, the trends to move form big urban downtown areas like New York, San Francisco, Seattle, Los Angeles and other similar locations will be reinforced. The trend of the remote workers moving to outlying suburban and rural communities will be strongly supported. This will also be enabled by the expansion of

high-speed Internet in rural areas, especially by the new Starlink satellite service.

3. Third, many individuals will continue to spend the money they "save" from not commuting and not paying high urban rents. Remote workers will continue to spend on enhancing their homes and home offices. They will continue to spend their money on home improvement products and buying the latest technology. This activity is already jamming supply chains because most of these products are manufactured in China. In addition, local wood prices have doubled because of the increase in Demand and a decrease in Supply because of lower harvesting and processing of wood during the Pandemic.

4. Fourth, there will be increased business demand for robust shortened supply chains, which will stimulate moving manufacturing activities from locations overseas to the North America trading area, Canada, Mexico and United States.

5. Restrictions and regulations on international travel may lessen, but these will not be entirely eliminated. After the initial Pandemic experience, the later endemic outbreaks of corona viruses and the widespread knowledge of the importance of scrupulous hygiene implies that some restrictions will endure. Even with some

lessening of international restrictions this will reinforce the shift towards domestic tourism.

6. The restrictions and regulations on travel along with the lower expenses of online meetings will discourage in-person conferences and conventions while most of these activities will remain online.

7. Demand for stockpiles of medical goods, supplies and personal protection equipment will be higher than before the Covid-19 Pandemic because of the experience of disruptions in global supply chains and foreign nations hoarding supplies. This higher level of demand will further push manufacturing of these products to the North America trading horizon of Canada, Mexico and United States.

8. Some degree of the social distancing designs for restaurants, shopping, entertainment and sports will become normal for large segments of the population, reinforcing the migration out of crowded urban areas to outlying suburban and rural locales.

9. The large number of remote workers will also create a new pool of remote learners, as many workers will be looking to improve their skills

and credentials to advance their careers in the new world of remote work.

10. The disruptions and dissatisfaction in urban crowded government schools of K-12 education will lead more parents to move their children to private schools and to rural communities where parents feel their children are safer and better served.

These changes and reinforced trends will ripple through the economy. Lower demands for gas and oil will proceed to more for electrical power in homes. Agriculture will become more organic and high-tech as we discussed in the section on Control Environment Agriculture (CEA). There will also be a demand for consultants who will help corporations to make their remote workers more productive and skilled by providing increased worker training, and increased management training, which will also make online conferences/conventions more productive and successful.

## Concluding Remarks

It is high time for most of us to prepare for living in the "New Normal." During the development phases, situations are in flux and we experience unexpected disturbances and shifts as the process continues toward a long-term equilibrium and steadiness. Nonetheless, individuals who have considered all the relevant factors have valuable knowledge of the direction and changes.

Grand changes in civilization are always disruptive. You have seen how pandemics produce far-reaching changes. Such evolutions in civilization appear throughout history, from the earliest eras when humans transitioned from hunter-gather to agriculture, and later from agrarian to the industrial-revolution and large cities.

In the past, these grand changes required that civilization could not turn backward to the former way of life before. People realized that these changes spawned new opportunities. In all cases, the discovery of new technology was involved. Now the technologies are more sophisticated, more powerful than ever before, and they will continue to evolve. People adopt the technologies and adapt to the new modes of living and working: The "New Normal." You need to align with the economic forces, do not revert to the comfort of the familiar.

**We are sailing on the seas of great change. We sincerely hope you enjoy your voyage, find the best anchorage, and land safely in a secure harbor of the "New Normal." New activities will replace the past, we have some good memories from times past, and going forward we will experience and witness new phenomena, which can also become favorite memories as the future becomes the past. The voyage will not be smooth, but bouncy and uneven, and there will**

be casualties. Nevertheless, for those who have a positive attitude, follow the directions on their "map" as the sail to their safe harbor in the "New Normal," the voyage through the Great Economic Transition will be remembered as an exciting time.

Bon Voyage!

Credit: Pexel – Matthew Barra

# REFERENCES & SELECTED READINGS

## References Chapter 1

Tappe, A (2020, November 18). *We're never going back to the old economy, Fed Chairman says.* CNN.com

https://edition.cnn.com/2020/11/17/economy/powell-economy-recovery/index.html

## References Chapter 2

Frederick, L.A. (1931). *Only Yesterday: an informal history of the nineteen-twenties.* Harper & Brothers, New York.

Hack, G. (2020, November 24). We're Celebrating Thanksgiving amid a Pandemic. Here's how we did it in 1918 – and what Happened next. USA Today

https://www.usatoday.com/indepth/news/nation/2020/11/21/covid-and thanksgiving-how-we-celebrated-during-1918-flu-Pandemic/6264231002/

History.com Editors (2020, April 1). Pandemics that Changed History. History.com.

https://www.history.com/topics/middle-ages/Pandemics-timeline

Klein, C. (2020, May 15). Why October 1918 Was America's Deadliest Month Ever. History.com.

https://www.history.com/news/spanish-flu-deaths-october-1918

Madriga, A. (2010, April 25). 1889 Pandemic Didn't Need Planes to Circle Globe in 4 Months. Wired Science https://web.archive.org/web/20100429163011/http://www.wired.com/wiredscience/2010/04/1889-russian-flu-Pandemic/

Roos, D. (2020, December 11). Why the 1918 Flu Pandemic Never Really Ended. History.com.

https://www.history.com/news/1918-flu-Pandemic-never-ended

Routt, D. (2020). The Economic Impact of the Black Death. Economic History Association.

https://eh.net/encyclopedia/the-economic-impact-of-the-black-death/

Vijgen, L., Keyaerts, E., Moës, E., Thoelen, I., Wollants, E., Lemey, P., Vandamme, A., Van Ranst, M. (2005). Complete Genomic Sequence of Human Coronavirus OC43: Molecular Clock Analysis Suggests a Relatively Recent Zoonotic Coronavirus Transmission Event. *Journal of Virology. 79* (3) 1595-1604

## References Chapter 3

Bosman, J. (2020, March 2). *Coronavirus Cases, Concentrated on the Coasts, Now Threaten America's Middle*. New York Times.
https://www.nytimes.com/2020/03/27/us/coronavirus-usa-midwest-south.html

Chappell, B., Romo, V. (2020, March 20). New York, Illinois Governors Issue Stay At Home Orders, Following California's Lead. National Public Radio.
https://www.npr.org/sections/coronavirus-live-updates/2020/03/20/818952589/coronavirus-n-y-gov-cuomo-says-100-of-workforce-must-stay-home

Crutsinger, M., Wiseman, P. (2020, November). Picture of US economy is worrisome as virus inflicts damage. Associated Press. https://apnews.com/article/Pandemics-jobless-claims-unemployment-coronavirus-Pandemic-economy-01d54b8c5f65a813a09df482aa4b6786

Hills, M. (2020, November 17). Covid-19 in the US: Is this coronavirus wave the worst yet? BBC World News.

https://www.bbc.com/news/world-us-canada-5496653

Neilson, S. Woodward, A. (2020, December 8). A comprehensive timeline of the coronavirus Pandemic at 12 months, from China's first case to the present. Business Insider

https://www.businessinsider.com/coronavirus-Pandemic-timeline-history-major-events-2020-3?op=

Rogers, E. M. (2003). Diffusion of Innovations (5th ed.). New York, New York, Free Press.

# References Chapter 4

Associated Press (2020, March 19). RoboPony: Chinese robot maker sees demand surge amid virus. AB-News.https://abcnews.go.com/Business/wireStory/robopony-chinese-robot-maker-sees-demand-surge-amid-69700762

Bach, Jonathan (2021, January 19) *"Nike leaves 280,000 square feet of Sunset Corridor real estate"* https://www.bizjournals.com/portland/news/2021/01/19/nike-vacates-280-000-square-feet-sunset-corridor.html

Baker, M. (2020, June 8). 9 Future of Work Trends Post-COVID-19. Gartner.com. https://www.gartner.com/smarterwithgartner/9-future-of-work-Bedord,

L. (2020, May 5). Experts predict challenges ahead for ag tech adoption. Agriculture.com. https://www.agriculture.com/news/technology/experts-predict-challenges-ahead-for-ag-tech-adoption

Brenan, M. (2020, April 3). U.S. Workers Discovering Affinity for Remote Work. Gallup. https://news.gallup.com/poll/306695/workers-discovering-affinity-remote-work.aspx https://buffer.com/state-of-remote-work-2019

Farshchi, S. (2020, April 10). Expect More Jobs And More Automation In The Post-COVID-19 Economy. Forbes.com. https://www.forbes.com/sites/shahinfarshchi/2020/04/10/expect-more-jobs-and-more-automation-in-the-post-covid-19-economy/?sh=50352e9929b4

Greig, J. (2020, April 13). Robots assisting factory workers and retailers in fight against coronavirus. Tech Republic.com. https://www.techrepublic.com/article/robots-assisting-factory-workers-and-retailers-in-fight-against-coronavirus/

Gullickson, G. (2020, July 10). *How the coronavirus Pandemic will accelerate digital agriculture*. Agriculture.com. https://www.agriculture.com/technology/crop-management/how-the-coronavirus-Pandemic-will-accelerate-digital-agriculture

Ravani, S. (2020, March 21). *Bay Area coronavirus decision: Behind the scenes of nation's first shelter-in-place order*. San Francisco Chronicle.
https://www.sfchronicle.com/bayarea/article/Bay-Area-coronavirus-decision-Behind-the-scenes-15148425.php

Secon, H., (2020, June 3). *An interactive map of the US cities and states still under lockdown — and those that are reopening*. Business Insider.https://www.businessinsider.com/us-map-stay-at-home-orders-lockdowns-2020-3

Levy, A. (2020, May 11). *Working from home is here to stay, even when the economy reopens.* CNBC.
https://www.cnbc.com/2020/05/11/work-from-home-is-here-to-stay-after-coronavirus.html

OWL Labs (2020). *State of Remote Work 2019*. OWL Labs.
https://www.owllabs.com/state-of-remote-work/2019

Rapoza, K. (2020, March 1). *Coronavirus Could Be The End Of China As A Global Manufacturing Hub.* Forbes.
https://www.forbes.com/sites/kenrapoza/2020/03/01/coronavirus-could-be-the-end-of-china-as-global-manufacturing-hub/?sh=1a4f85bb5298

Sents, N. (2020, June 3). *Post-COVID-19 Pandemic: What's it mean for agriculture?* Agriculture.com
https://www.agriculture.com/news/business/post-covid-19-Pandemic-what-s-it-mean-for-agriculture

Straitstimes (2020, March 30). *Pandemic speeds up iPhone makers' plans to exit China*. The Straits Timestrends-post-covid-19/
https://www.straitstimes.com/business/economy/Pandemic-speeds-up-iphone-makers-plans-to-exit-china

Sutherland, B., (2020, May 15). *Future of Factories Is More Robots and More Mexico.* Bloomberg

.https://www.bloomberg.com/opinion/articles/2020-05-15/coronavirus-future-of-factories-is-more-robots-and-more-mexico

"Sewage-testing robots process wastewater faster to predict COVID-19 outbreaks sooner" https://theconversation.com/sewage-testing-robots-process-wastewater-faster-to-predict-covid-19-outbreaks-sooner-156467?utm

Wong M., (2020, June 29). *Stanford research provides a snapshot of a new working-from-home economy.* Stanford University.https://news.stanford.edu/2020/06/29/snapshot-new-working-home-economy/ Buffer.com (2020). State of Remote Work 2019. Buffer.com.

# References Chapter 5

Abrams, Z. (2020, October 1). The future of remote work: When it's done right, telework can improve employee productivity, creativity and morale, psychologists' research finds. American Psychological Association. https://www.apa.org/monitor/2019/10/cover-remote-work

Altig, D., Robertson, J. (2020, May 28). *Firms Expect Working from Home to Triple.* Federal Reserve Bank https://www.frbatlanta.org/blogs/macroblog/2020/05/28/firms-expect-working-from-home-to-triple

Attanasio, C. (2020, November 23). Cut off: School closings leave rural students isolated. Associated Press. https://apnews.com/article/technology-new-mexico-

Bahr, L. (2020, December 2). The Sundance Film Festival goes largely virtual for 2021. Komonews.com. https://komonews.com/news/coronavirus/the-sundance-film-festival-goes-largely-virtual-for-2021

Bakhtiari, K. (2020, May 18). How Will The Pandemic Change Consumer Behavior. Forbes https://www.forbes.com/sites/kianbakhtiari/2020/05/18/how-will-the-Pandemic-change-consumer-behavior/?sh=a39b22066f6a

Baldwin, A. (2020, March 22). Virtual world races to fill sporting void left by coronavirus. Reuters. https://www.weforum.org/agenda/2020/03/virtual-world-races-to-fill-sporting-void-left-by-coronavirus

Bearne, S. (2020, November 17). Entertainers find new ways to pay the bills. BBC News https://www.bbc.com/news/business-54870757

Billock, J. (2020, September 2). Want to Support Wildlife Conservation in Africa? Start by Going on a Virtual Safari. Smithsonian Magazine. https://www.smithsonianmag.com/travel/want-to-support-wildlife-conservation-in-africa-start-by-going-on-virtual-safari-180975656/

Bloom, N. (2020, June). How working from home works out. Sanford Institute for Economic Policy Research. https://siepr.stanford.edu/research/publications/how-working-home-works-out

Brenan, M., (2020, April 3). U.S. Workers Discovering Affinity for Remote Work. Gallup.com https://news.gallup.com/poll/306695/workers-discovering-affinity-remote-work.aspx

Brown, D. (2020, November 17). Coronavirus: How to be happier while working from home. BBC News. https://www.bbc.com/news/uk-54886125

Epstein, A. (2020, September 28). Game on: How COVID-19 became the perfect match for gamers. Quartz.https://www.weforum.org/agenda/2020/09/covid19-coronavirus-Pandemic-video-games-entertainment-media/

Farrer, L. (2020, May 12). The New Normal Isn't Remote Work. It's Better. Forbes. https://www.forbes.com/sites/laurelfarrer/2020/05/12/the-new-normal-isnt-remote-work-its-better/?sh=29dd7df22405

Friedman, U. (2020, May 1). I Have Seen the Future—And It's Not the Life We Knew. The Atlantic. https://www.theatlantic.comm/politics/archive/2020/05/life-after-coronavirus-china-denmark-south-korea/611011/

Hall, S. (2020, May 7). This is how COVID-19 is affecting the musicindustry. World Economic Forum. https://www.weforum.org/agenda/2020/05/this-is-how-covid-19-is-affecting-the-music-industry

Hall, S. (2020, May 15). How COVID-19 is taking gaming and esports to the next level. World Economic Forum. https://www.weforum.org/agenda/2020/05/covid-19-taking-gaming-and-esports-next-level

Hall, S., Pasquini, S. (2020, July 23). Can there be a fairy-tale ending for Hollywood after COVID-19? World Economic Forum. https://www.weforum.org/agenda/2020/07/impact-coronavirus-covid-19-hollywood-global-film-industry-movie-theatres/

Hepler, L. (2020, August 28). Blackboard brawl: How California's teachers hope to avoid 60,000 layoffs. Cal Matters.

https://calmatters.org/education/2020/08/california-teachers-crisis-layoffs/?

Hou, C. (2020, July 1). The advantages and disadvantages of online learning during the coronavirus Pandemic. The Hill. https://thehill.com/changing-america/well-being/prevention-cures/505452-the-advantages-and-disadvantages-of-online

Kennedy, M. (2020, December 3). Theater uses its creativity to defy Pandemic and stage shows. Associated Press. https://apnews.com/article/Pandemics-new-york-theater-coronavirus-Pandemic-manhattan-f7ccd7388ec416bb9aa8216aeb0cc954

Ingraham, C. (2018, August 30). These 3 charts show the rapid rise of eSports. Washington Post. https://www.weforum.org/agenda/2018/08/the-massive-popularity-of-esports-in-charts

Ingraham, C. (2019, October 7). Nine days on the road. Average commute time reached a new record last year. Washington Post. https://www.washingtonpost.com/business/2019/10/07/nine-days-road-average-commute-time-reached-new-record-last-year/

Japan Times (2020, August 10). Kyoto railway attracting future passengers with virtual trips. The Japan Times. https://www.japantimes.co.jp/news/2020/08/19/business/corporate-business/kyoto-railway-coronavirus-trips/

Kirka, D. Lindsey, B. (2020, October 5). Hundreds of Regal, Cineworld movie theaters to close. ABC News. https://abcnews.go.com/Business/wireStory/hundreds-regal-cineworld-movie-theaters-close-73425901

Levy, A. (2020, May 11). Working from home is here to stay, even when the economy reopens. CNBC https://www.cnbc.com/2020/05/11/work-from-home-is-here-to-stay-after-coronavirus.html

Lufkin, B., Myska, S., Shebbeare, S. (2020, October 7). The remote work experiment that upped productivity 13%. BBC News. https://www.bbc.com/worklife/article/20200710-the-remote-work-experiment-that-made-staff-more-productive

Perino, M. (2019, July 18). Here's what the average person spends on their commute annually in every state. Business Insider. https://www.businessinsider.com/average-spending-on-commute-how-much-money-2019-7?op=1

Rockerman, O. (2020, October 1). Free to Work Remotely, Young Americans Are Covid Road Tripping. Bloomberg. https://www.bloomberg.com/news/articles/2020-10-01/covid-news-remote-work-lets-young-americans-take-road-trips?utm_source=pocket-newtab

Roos, D. (2020, April 28). When WWI, Pandemic and Slump Ended, Americans Sprung Into the Roaring Twenties. History.com. https://www.history.com/news/Pandemic-world-war-i-roaring-twenties

Rosales, G. (2020, November 22). Climbing Mount Everest in New Mexico. Albuquerque Journal. https://www.abqjournal.com/1519929/climbing-mount-everest-in-new-mexico-ex-local-athletes-find-everesting-a-good-way-to-train-or-simply-pass-the-time-during-the-Pandemic.html

Sherman, A. (2020, December 3). WarnerMedia CEO Jason Kilar doesn't think he just destroyed the movie theater industry. CNBC. https://www.cnbc.com/2020/12/03/warnermedia-ceo-jason-kilar-doesnt-think-he-destroyed-movie-theaters.html

VADALA, N. (2020, July 2). 12 drive-in movie theaters near Philly. The Philadelphia Inquirer. https://www.inquirer.com/things-to-do/drive-in-movie-theaters-pennsylvania-new-jersey-delaware-20200627.html

WABC (2020, November 18). MTA unveils 'doomsday' budget with massive cuts, citing lack of federal funding. WABC News. https://www.msn.com/en-us/news/politics/mta-unveils-doomsday-budget-with-massive-cuts-citing-lack-of-federal-funding/ar-BB1b7Rdj

Westfall, C. (2020, May 20). New Survey Shows 47% Increase In Productivity: 3 Things You Must Do When Working From Home. Forbes. https://www.forbes.com/sites/chriswestfall/2020/05/20/new-survey-shows-47-increase-in-productivity-3-things-you-must-do-when-working-from-home/?sh=5001d8dc80dc

Wu, K. J. (2020, April 20). Explore Washington, D.C. From Home With This Free, Smithsonian Scholar-Led Tour. Smithsonian Magazine.

https://www.smithsonianmag.com/smart-news/tour-washington-dc-home-great-tours-now-free-all-180974706/

# References Chapter 6

Armstrong, D., Goldman, H., Chukey, K. (2020, May 28). *Why New York Suffered When Other Cities Were Spared by Covid-19.* Bloomberg News.

https://www.bloomberg.com/news/articles/2020-05-28/why-was-new-york-hit-so-badly-with-covid-19

BBC (2020, October 28). *Boeing to cut 20% of workforce by end of 2021*. BBC News. https://www.bbc.com/news/business-54716296

Bosman, J. (2020, March 2). *Coronavirus Cases, Concentrated on the Coasts, Now Threaten America's Middle*. New York Times. https://www.nytimes.com/2020/03/27/us/coronavirus-usa-midwest-south.html

Broom, D. (2020, July 30). Could this COVID-19 'health passport' be the future of travel and events? Business Insider. https://www.weforum.org/agenda/2020/07/covid-19-passport-app-health-travel-covidpass-quarantine-event/

BUSSEWITZ, C. (2020, December 10). *Fears and tension mount for commuters still heading to work*. Associated Press. https://apnews.com/article/new-york-health-transportation-coronavirus-Pandemic-98c309f705004e22a6d1832e96a1014d

Cruise Critic Staff (2020, December 15). *When Are Cruise Lines Around the World Expected To Resume Service?* Cruise Critic. https://www.cruisecritic.com/news/5206/

DiFurio, D., Arnold, K. (2020, November 24). *Dallas hotels hit hard by COVID see massive drops in revenue and reservations as holidays loom*. Dallas Morning News. https://www.dallasnews.com/business/local-companies/2020/11/24/dallas-hotels-hit-hard-by-covid-see-massive-drops-in-revenue-and-reservations-as-holidays-loom/

Editorial Staff (2020, December 1). *COVID-19: Impact on Trucking Companies, Economy and Trade*. Verizon Connect. https://www.verizonconnect.com/resources/article/covid-19-trucking-impact/

Ellis, N. T. (2020, April 8). *"An essential service": Amtrak, Greyhound continue routes despite coronavirus cases*. USA Today. https://www.usatoday.com/story/travel/2020/04/08/amtrak-greyhound-continue-routes-despite-coronavirus-cases-board/5111338002/

Fisher, J. (2020, October 1). *ATA's Costello: 'The recession is over'*. Fleet Owner. https://www.fleetowner.com/covid-19-coverage/article/21143457/trucking-economist-the-covid-recession-is-over-a-new-consumer-is-born

Fitzsimmons, E.G. (2018, August 1). *Subway Ridership Dropped Again in New York as Passengers Flee to Uber*. New York Times. http://www.nytimes.com/2018/08/01/nyregion/subway-ridership-nyc-metro.html

Freightos (2020, December 1). *How Coronavirus is Impacting Shipping: Air Cargo, Ocean Freight, Trucking, and More.* https://www.freightos.com/freight-resources/coronavirus-updates/

Frishberg, H. (2020, October 12). *Luxury cruise ships being scrapped for metal amid ongoing Pandemic.* New York Post. https://nypost.com/2020/10/12/luxury-cruise-ships-being-scrapped-for-metal-amid-ongoing-Pandemic/

Holland, J. (2020, March 1). *Coronavirus: Could It Destroy the Cruise Ship Industry?* National Interest. https://nationalinterest.org/blog/buzz/coronavirus-could-it-destroy-cruise-ship-industry-127552

IATA (2020, July 1). *Air Cargo Market Analysis*. International Air Transportation Association. https://www.iata.org/en/pressroom/pr/2020-08-31-01/

KOMO News Staff (2020, September 30). *Report: Boeing to move 787 Dreamliner assembly in Everett to South Carolina*. KOMO News. https://komonews.com/news/local/report-boeing-to-move-787-dreamliner-assembly-in-everett-to-south-carolina

KOMO News Staff (2020, December 3). *'Brutal news': Seattle hotels have lowest occupancy on West Coast amid Pandemic*. KOMO News. https://komonews.com/news/local/brutal-news-seattle-hotels-have-lowest-occupancy-on-west-coast-amid-Pandemic

Marchant, N. (2020, November 6). *COVID-19 on the cruise industry*. World Economic Forum. https://www.weforum.org/agenda/2020/11/impact-coronavirus-Pandemic-cruise-ships/

Martin, H. (2020, March 10). *Will the Coronavirus Outbreak Sink the Industry?* Los Angeles Times. https://www.latimes.com/business/story/2020-03-10/coronavirus-cruise-industry

Meyer, D. (2020, April 16). *MTA expects low end-of-year ridership, wants another coronavirus bailout*. New York Post. https://nypost.com/2020/04/16/mta-expects-low-end-of-year-ridership-wants-another-bailout/

Meyer, D. (2020, September 4). *Subway ridership tops 1.5 million for first time since start of COVID-19*. New York Post. https://nypost.com/2020/09/04/subway-ridership-tops-1-5-million-for-first-time-since-covid-19/

Mocker, G. (2020, November 11). *NYC Transit faces challenges in the short and long terms*. PIX11.com. https://www.pix11.com/news/local-news/nyc-transit-faces-challenges-in-the-short-and-long-terms

Mutasa, T. (2020, November 14). *After the COVID-19 Pandemic will you still wear a mask on flights?* KOMO News. https://komonews.com/news/coronavirus/after-the-covid-19-Pandemic-will-you-still-wear-a-mask-on-flights

Ott M. (2020, November 3). *Cruise industry throws in the towel on 2020, looks to 2021*. Associated Press. https://apnews.com/article/virus-outbreak-sailing-4f8ed01fc0f6efcda12356a033845494

Peltz, J. (2020, November 23). *Tourists few, NY gift shops struggle but don't lose (heart)*. Associated Press. https://apnews.com/article/new-york-coronavirus-Pandemic-dd097c35f830f0807774bf42b1b10c8b

Phan S. (2020, November 14). *Restaurants brace themselves for more COVID-19 restrictions*. KOMO News. https://komonews.com/news/local/restaurants-brace-themselves-for-more-covid-19-restrictions

Quirmbach, C. (2020, November 25). *Amtrak Trains Operating To Milwaukee During Pandemic, But With Reduced Ridership*. WUWM.com. https://www.wuwm.com/post/amtrak-trains-operating-milwaukee-during-Pandemic-reduced-ridership#stream/0

Rail News (2020, November 30). *U.S. rail traffic climbs on intermodal gain in Week 47*. Progressive Railroading. https://www.progressiverailroading.com/rail_industry_trends/news/US-rail-traffic-climbs-on-intermodal-gain-in-Week-47--62154

Rail News (2020, May 1). *From the Editor: While uncertainty rules, railroads prep for recovery.* Progressive Railroading. https://www.progressiverailroading.com/rail_industry_trends/article/From-the-Editor-While-uncertainty-rules-railroads-prep-for-recovery--60385

Rust, S. (2020, May 10). *Freight industry takes hits during the Pandemic, but the trains keep chugging along*. Los Angeles Times. https://www.latimes.com/california/story/2020-05-10/coronavirus-hammers-freight-rail-industry-but-trains-still-roll

Smith J. R. (2020, May 1). *What's in store for the cruise industry?* CNN. https://www.cnn.com/travel/article/cruise-industry-coronavirus-aftermath/index.html

Smith, S. (2020, April 17). *Coronavirus has hit the trucking industry 'like a brick wall'*. Yahoo. https://news.yahoo.com/coronavirus-trucking-industry-economy-retail-ceo-grocery-173116971.html

Street, F. (2020, August 25). *Cruise trips are back. This is what they look like now.* CNN.

https://www.cnn.com/travel/article/future-of-cruising-coronavirus/index.html

Transportation Topics (2020, September 3). *Trucking Surges as Capacity Tightens Amid Continued Pandemic*. Transportation Topics News. https://www.ttnews.com/articles/trucking-surges-capacity-tightens-amid-continued-Pandemic

Trucker News Staff (2020, December 3). *Preliminary reports show 'explosion' of Class 8 truck orders in November*. The Trucker News. https://www.thetrucker.com/trucking-news/equipment-tech/preliminary-reports-show-explosion-of-class-8-truck-orders-in-november

Walker, J. (2020, August 31). *The USPS and U.S. transit agencies face the same impossible demand: Succeed as both a business and a public service.* Bloomberg.

https://www.bloomberg.com/news/articles/2020-08-31/how-public-transit-is-like-the-postal-service?srnd=citylab

# References Chapter 7

Associated Press (2020, March 19). RoboPony: *Chinese robot maker sees demand surge amid virus.* Associated Press. https://abcnews.go.com/Business/wireStory/robopony-chinese-robot-maker-sees-demand-surge-amid-69700762

Bakhtiari, K. (2020, August 24). *Why Consumer Behavior Has Reached 2030 Levels*. Forbes. https://www.forbes.com/sites/kianbakhtiari/2020/08/24/why-consumer-behavior-has-reached-2030-levels/?sh=41cc0690256b

Bedord, L. (2020, May 5). *Experts predict challenges ahead for ag tech adoption*. Agriculture.com https://www.agriculture.com/news/technology/experts-predict-challenges-ahead-for-ag-tech-adoption

Burch, W. (2020, November 28). *Black Friday hits new record online as U.S. shoppers stay home during Pandemic*. KTLA.com. https://ktla.com/news/nationworld/black-friday-hits-new-record-online-as-u-s-shoppers-stay-home-during-Pandemic/

Danziger, P. N. (2020, April 7). *Walmart Leads The Soon-To-Be $35 Billion Curbside Pickup Market*. Forbes. https://www.forbes.com/sites/pamdanziger/2019/04/07/walmart-is-in-the-lead-in-the-soon-to-be-35-billion-curbside-pickup-market/?sh=59205299199e

DeMuro, R. (2020, December 2). *Watch this robotic barista whip up a Boba tea drink in less than two minutes*. KTLA.com. https://ktla.com/morning-news/technology/bobacino-robot-boba-tea-bar-demo-richontech/

Dunn, K. (2020, April 20). *'Unreal': Oil prices go negative for the first time in history*. Fortune https://fortune.com/2020/04/20/oil-prices-negative-crash-price-crude-market/

Editor, (2020, December 2). *World coal market: brief overview*. The Coal Hub. https://thecoalhub.com/world-coal-market-brief-overview-10.html

Editorial Department (2020, December 4). *The End Of Growth For U.S. Shale*. OilPrice.com https://oilprice.com/Energy/Energy-General/The-End-Of-Growth-For-US-Shale.html

Ehrhardt, M. (2020, August 5). *Logitech on Webcam Shortage: "We're Doing Everything We Can"*. TomsHardware.com. https://www.theverge.com/2020/4/9/21199521/webcam-shortage-price-raise-logitech-razer-amazon-best-buy-ebay

Evans, M. (2020, May 19). *7 Predictions For How COVID-19 Will Change Retail In The Future*. Forbes.

https://www.forbes.com/sites/michelleevans1/2020/05/19/7-predictions-for-how-covid-19-will-change-retail-in-the-future/?sh=4332c13a5be3

Evans, M. (2020, June 2). *What To Consider When Selecting Tech To Help Adapt To The New Normal.* Forbes. https://www.forbes.com/sites/michelleevans1/2020/06/02/tech-that-will-improve-commerce-in-the-near--and-long-term/?sh=39341cce2563

Farrer, L. (2020, May 14). *The Tools That Will Power The Remote Work Revolution.* Forbes. https://www.forbes.com/sites/laurelfarrer/2020/05/14/the-tools-that-will-power-the-remote-work-revolution/?sh=68df9b9aa4c5

Farshchi, S., (2020, April 10). *Expect More Jobs And More Automation In The Post-COVID-19 Economy.* Forbes https://www.forbes.com/sites/shahinfarshchi/2020/04/10/expect-more-jobs-and-more-automation-in-the-post-covid-19-economy/?sh=50352e9929b4

Greig, J. (2020, April 13). *Robots assisting factory workers and retailers in fight against coronavirus.* Tech Republic. https://www.techrepublic.com/article/robots-assisting-factory-workers-and-retailers-in-fight-against-coronavirus/

Gullickson, G. (2020, July 10). *How the coronavirus Pandemic will accelerate digital agriculture.* Agriculture.com https://www.agriculture.com/technology/crop-management/how-the-coronavirus-Pandemic-will-accelerate-digital-agriculture

Iqbal, M. (2020, October 30). *Zoom Revenue and Usage Statistics (2020).* Businessofapps.com https://www.businessofapps.com/data/zoom-statistics/

Kohan, S. E. (2020, May 19). *Walmart's Online Sales Have Surged 74% During The Pandemic.* Forbes.

https://www.forbes.com/sites/shelleykohan/2020/05/19/walmart-revenue-up-86-e-commerce-up-74/?sh=3dee0c5d66cc

Levy, A. (2020, May 11). *Working from home is here to stay, even when the economy reopens.* CNBC https://www.cnbc.com/2020/05/11/work-from-home-is-here-to-stay-after-coronavirus.html

Lyons, K. (2020, October 11). *After an early Pandemic shortage computers are shipping again, Canalys reports*. The Verge https://www.theverge.com/2020/10/11/21511425/laptops-desktops-shipping-Pandemic-apple-dell-lenovo-hp-acer

Mikulskia, A. (2020, April 1). *(Natural Gas Markets Beyond COVID-19.* Forbes. https://www.forbes.com/sites/thebakersinstitute/2020/04/01/natural-gas-markets-beyond-covid-19/?sh=37288aa654c4

Morgan, B. (2020, June 8). *5 Examples Of What Post-COVID Retail Will Look Like*. Forbes. https://www.forbes.com/sites/blakemorgan/2020/06/08/5-examples-of-what-post-covid-retail-will-look-like/?sh=5684689c524e

Glaeser, E. (2011). *Triumph of the City: How Our Greatest Invention Makes Us Richer, Smarter, Greener, Healthier and Happier*. Penguin Books.

Morris, B. (2020, November 13). *Robots to take on more supermarket tasks*. BBC News. https://www.bbc.com/news/business-54902518

Rapoza, K. (2020, March 1). *Coronavirus Could Be The End Of China As A Global Manufacturing Hub.* Forbes https://www.forbes.com/sites/kenrapoza/2020/03/01/coronavirus-could-be-the-end-of-china-as-global-manufacturing-hub/?sh=1a4f85bb5298

Schaeffer, J., and Turnbull A. (2020, December 1). *Glimmers of hope for world economy, but dangers lurk*. Associated Press.

https://apnews.com/article/europe-economic-outlook-health-coronavirus-Pandemic-economy-790aac53128f3adcbde9f82af3c98114

Sents, N. (2020, June 3). *Post-COVID-19 Pandemic: What's it mean for agriculture?* Agriculture.com https://www.agriculture.com/news/business/post-covid-19-Pandemic-what-s-it-mean-for-agriculture

Slav, I. (2020, December 3). *Saudi Oil Exports To U.S. Slump To 35-Year Low.* OilPrice.com   https://oilprice.com/Latest-Energy-News/World-News/Saudi-Oil-Exports-To-US-Slump-To-35-Year-Low.html

Smith, S. (2020, April 17). *Low oil prices is 'a train wreck in full speed': Parsley Energy CEO.* Yahoo Finance. https://finance.yahoo.com/news/parsley-energy-ceo-low-oil-prices-coronavirus-texas-opec-train-wreck-in-full-speed-114505751.html

Staff (2018). *A Brief History of Video Conferencing From 1964 to 2017.* Eztalks.com   https://www.eztalks.com/video-conference/history-of-video-conferencing.html

Staff (2020, April 16). *Impact of COVID-19 on the Video Conferencing Market, 2020.* Researchandmarkets.com. https://www.businesswire.com/news/home/20200416005739/en/Impact-of-COVID-19-on-the-Video-Conferencing-Market-2020---ResearchAndMarkets.com

Staff (2020, April 30). *Oil Market Report - April 2020.* International Energy Agency.  https://www.iea.org/reports/oil-market-report-april-2020

Stern, M. (2020, March 24). *Retailers are going to curbside and delivery. Will they stay that way?* Retail Wire. https://retailwire.com/discussion/retailers-are-going-to-curbside-and-delivery-will-they-stay-that-way/

Stevens, P. (2020, April 30). *Energy demand, hit by coronavirus crisis, is set to see record drop this year*. IEA says. CNBC. https://www.cnbc.com/2020/04/30/energy-demand-set-to-fall-the-most-on-record-this-year-amid-coronavirus-Pandemic-iea-says.html

Sullivan, B. (2020, April 26). *Why oil prices went negative and why they can go negative again*. CNBC. https://www.cnbc.com/2020/04/26/why-oil-prices-went-negative-and-why-they-can-go-negative-again.html

Sutherland, B., (2020, May 15). *Future of Factories Is More Robots and More Mexico.* Bloomberg. https://www.bloomberg.com/opinion/articles/2020-05-15/coronavirus-future-of-factories-is-more-robots-and-more-mexico

Welch, C. (2020, April 9). *Webcams have become impossible to find, and prices are skyrocketing.* The Verge. https://www.theverge.com/2020/4/9/21199521/webcam-shortage-price-raise-logitech-razer-amazon-best-buy-ebay

Whipple, T. (2020, December 4). *Peak Oil Is Suddenly Upon Us.* Energy Bulletin. https://daily.energybulletin.org/2020/12/peak-oil-is-suddenly-upon-us/

# Reference Chapter 8

Associated Press (2020, October 3). Some coastal residents choosing northern Michigan amid virus. Associated Press. https://apnews.com/article/virus-outbreak-freedom-of-information-act-michigan-traverse-city-voting-2020-13e8288a2a915799489a6f88ef176d21

Associated Press (2020, December 3). Seattle rents down 20% since start of COVID-19 Pandemic. KOMO News https://komonews.com/news/local/seattle-rents-down-20-since-start-of-covid-19-Pandemic

Bach, T. (2020, June 29). What the Surge in Working From Home Means for Big Cities. U.S. News. https://www.usnews.com/news/cities/articles/2020-06-29/how-teleworking-may-accelerate-the-shift-away-from-big-cities

Berliner, U. (2020, June 22). Get A Comfortable Chair: Permanent Work From Home Is Coming. National Public Radio. https://www.npr.org/2020/06/22/870029658/get-a-comfortable-chair-permanent-work-from-home-is-coming

Berliner, U. (2020, July 8). New Yorkers Look To Suburbs And Beyond. Other City Dwellers May Be Next. National Public Radio.

https://www.npr.org/2020/07/08/887585383/new-yorkers-look-to-suburbs-and-beyond-other-city-dwellers-may-be-next

Byers, D. (2020, May 12). Twitter employees can work from home forever, CEO says. NBC News. https://www.nbcnews.com/tech/tech-news/twitter-employees-can-work-home-forever-ceo-says-n1205346

CDC Staff (2020, December 18). COVID-19 in Children and Teens. Centers for Disease Control and Prevention. https://www.cdc.gov/coronavirus/2019-ncov/daily-life-coping/children/symptoms.html

CDC Staff (2020, August 18). COVID-19 Hospitalization and Death by Age. Centers for Disease Control and Prevention. https://www.cdc.gov/coronavirus/2019-ncov/daily-life-coping/children/symptoms.html

De Lea, B. (2020, June 3). Wealthy coronavirus rush hits 'forgotten' towns of Long Island, as Hamptons inventory dries up. Fox

Business. https://www.foxbusiness.com/real-estate/coronavirus-rush-gold-coast-long-island

De Lea, B. (2020, August 28). Hamptons businesses seizing economic opportunity as NYC residents extend stays. Fox Business. https://www.foxbusiness.com/lifestyle/hamptons-businesses-opportunity-nyc-residents-stay

De Lea, B. (2020, September 2). New York exodus accelerates amid Pandemic as some residents head south. Fox Business. https://www.foxbusiness.com/real-estate/nyc-move-outs-surge-Pandemic

De Lea, B. (2020, October 13). Expensive-city exodus leads to massive rent declines in NYC, San Francisco. Fox Business. https://www.foxbusiness.com/real-estate/expensive-city-exodus-rent-declines-nyc-san-francisco

De Lea, B. (2020, October 29). Millions of Americans plan to move to more affordable areas amid Pandemic. Fox Business. https://www.foxbusiness.com/luxury/millions-americans-move-affordable-areas-Pandemic

Genovese, D. (2020, November 13). Tech hub rentals lose luster as coronavirus fuels urban exodus. Fox Business. https://www.foxbusiness.com/real-estate/tech-hubs-losing-luster-as-remote-work-takes-over

Fox, M., LaMotte, S. (2020, November 16). Over 1 million US children have been diagnosed with COVID-19, pediatricians say. ABC 7 News. https://abc7ny.com/kids-with-coronavirus-kid-covid-symptoms-cases-of/8019708/

Geraghty, J. (2020, April 23). Moving Out and Not Coming Back. National Review. https://www.nationalreview.com/the-morning-jolt/moving-out-and-not-coming-back/

Glaeser, E. (2011). Triumph of the City: How Our Greatest Invention Makes Us Richer, Smarter, Greener, Healthier and Happier. Penguin Books.

Haag, M. (2020, May 12). Manhattan Faces a Reckoning if Working From Home Becomes the Norm. New York Times. https://www.nytimes.com/2020/05/12/nyregion/coronavirus-work-from-home.html

Hubbard, K. (2020, October 15). New York City's Falling Rents Reflect the Pain of COVID-19. U.S. News. https://www.usnews.com/news/cities/articles/2020-10-15/new-york-citys-falling-rents-reflect-the-trauma-of-covid-19

Kailath, R. (2020, September 1). 'Do I Really Need This Much Office Space?' Pandemic Emptied Buildings, But How Long? National Public Radio. https://www.npr.org/2020/09/01/906767790/do-i-really-need-this-much-office-space-Pandemic-emptied-buildings-but-how-long

Kim, S. (2020, December 22). U.S. Child COVID Cases Sees 'Highest Weekly Increase Since Pandemic Began'. Newsweek. https://www.msn.com/en-us/news/us/us-child-covid-cases-sees-highest-weekly-increase-since-Pandemic-began/ar-BB1c93yO

Khazan, O. (2020, May 4). Work From Home Is Here to Stay. The Atlantic.

https://www.theatlantic.com/health/archive/2020/05/work-from-home-Pandemic/611098/

Kiesnoski, K. (2020, May 10). Travel changed after 9/11; Here's how it will look after the Covid-19 Pandemic finally recedes. CNBC. https://www.cnbc.com/2020/05/10/heres-how-travel-will-change-after-the-covid-19-Pandemic-recedes.html

Klein, M. (2020. August 11). New Yorkers keep moving out of the city to suburbs, other states. New York Post. https://nypost.com/2020/08/11/new-yorkers-flee-nyc-in-droves/

Klein, M. (2020, November 21). See where all the people leaving New York are moving to. New York Post. https://nypost.com/2020/11/21/where-people-leaving-new-york-are-moving/

Long, S. (2020, August 11). Coronavirus: Can California's economy survive the latest surge? BBC News. https://www.bbc.com/news/world-us-canada-53604621

Madyun, H. (2020, November 19). Francisco in apparent Pandemic exodus. News Nation. https://www.newsnationnow.com/us-news/west/people-businesses-moving-out-of-san-francisco-in-apparent-Pandemic-exodus/

Manfredi, L. (2020, November 24). Home buyers pivot back to urban cities, rural areas still hot. Fox Business. https://www.foxbusiness.com/economy/home-buyers-pivot-back-to-urban-cities-rural-areas-still-hot

Perez, R. (2020, September 9). Would You Move to a Zoom Town? Domino.com.   https://www.domino.com/content/zoom-towns-real-estate-trend/

Rapoza, K. (2020, June 12). Start Spreading The News, New Yorkers Are Leaving Today. Forbes. https://www.forbes.com/sites/kenrapoza/2020/06/11/new-york-realestate-miami-exodus-Pandemic-and-protests/?sh=43256af955dc

Rosalsky, G. (2020, September 8). Zoom Towns And The New Housing Market For The 2 Americas. National Public Radio. https://www.npr.org/sections/money/2020/09/08/909680016/zoom-towns-and-the-new-housing-market-for-the-2-americas

Shepard, G. (2020, September 28). How Remote Work Can Transform Smaller Cities. U.S. News. https://www.usnews.com/news/cities/articles/2020-09-28/what-remote-working-means-for-second-tier-cities

New York Post Staff, (2020, November 15). New Yorkers flee city in droves amid coronavirus, crime concerns: report. Fox Business. https://www.foxbusiness.com/real-estate/new-yorkers-flee-city-amid-rising-coronavirus-crime-concerns-report

WABC (2020, November 18). MTA unveils 'doomsday' budget with massive cuts, citing lack of federal funding. WABC News. https://www.msn.com/en-us/news/politics/mta-unveils-doomsday-budget-with-massive-cuts-citing-lack-of-federal-funding/ar-BB1b7Rdj

Wong M., (2020, June 29). Stanford research provides a snapshot of a new working-from-home economy. Stanford University. https://news.stanford.edu/2020/06/29/snapshot-new-working-home-economy

## References Chapter 9

Mitry, D. (2017), Economic Secrets & Surprises: the Matrix Economy https://www.amazon.com/Economic-Secrets-Surprises-Matrix-Economy/dp/1979832803/

Smith, A. (1776), An Inquiry Into The Nature And Causes Of The Wealth Of Nations: Complete Five Unabridged Books. Amazon Books Amazon.com

*The Economist* December 2020.

## References Chapter 10

Anez, G., Massey, M. (2020, November 29). *Millions of Americans have strongly considered changing career paths during*

*Pandemic, study says*. KSAT.com
https://www.ksat.com/news/local/2020/11/29/millions-of-americans-have-strongly-considered-changing-career-paths-during-Pandemic-study-says/

Hess, A. (2020, December 14). *27% of Teachers Are Considering Quitting Because of Covid, Survey Finds*. CNBC
https://www.nbcsandiego.com/news/business/money-report/27-of-teachers-are-considering-quitting-because-of-covid-survey-finds/2470651/

Tappe, A (2020, November 18). *We're never going back to the old economy, Fed Chairman says.* CNN.com
https://edition.cnn.com/2020/11/17/economy/powell-economy-recovery/index.html

# FOR READERS' PERSONAL NOTES

# FOR READERS' PERSONAL NOTES

www.ingramcontent.com/pod-product-compliance
Lightning Source LLC
Chambersburg PA
CBHW071355210526
45465CB00001B/106